A Thesaurus of Women

To Linda
Strong Women's Wishes

Barbara Joan Zeitz
2014

A Thesaurus of Women

From Cherry Blossoms to Cell Phones

Barbara Joan Zeitz, MA

iUniverse, Inc.
Bloomington

A Thesaurus of Women
From Cherry Blossoms to Cell Phones

iUniverse books may be ordered through booksellers or by contacting:

iUniverse
1663 Liberty Drive
Bloomington, IN 47403
www.iuniverse.com
1-800-Authors (1-800-288-4677)

Because of the dynamic nature of the Internet, any web addresses or links contained in this book may have changed since publication and may no longer be valid. The views expressed in this work are solely those of the author and do not necessarily reflect the views of the publisher, and the publisher hereby disclaims any responsibility for them.

Any people depicted in stock imagery provided by Thinkstock are models, and such images are being used for illustrative purposes only.

Certain stock imagery © Thinkstock.

ISBN: 978-1-4620-6865-4 (sc)
ISBN: 978-1-4620-6867-8 (hc)
ISBN: 978-1-4620-6866-1 (e)

Printed in the United States of America

iUniverse rev. date: 01/18/2012

Dedicated to
and in
appreciation of
all women unable to be, to learn, to do
all they could
because they were women.

Contents

Preface

~

*A*t the turn of the century, this new century twenty-one, I was a seasoned (not yet a senior) adult student pursuing my graduate degree in women's studies. As I read, researched, and wrote women's history, I learned much about my history as a woman that I did not know. And as I began to know more, I began to realize that there was yet so much more to know.

Upon receiving my master's degree in women's studies in 2003, I began giving lectures and writing an online column to acknowledge women and their accomplishments viewed through the lens of gender. My work revealed how women's history greatly affects the lives of men and women today and how so little is shared or celebrated about women and their significant accomplishments.

In all my lectures, to emphasize this atrocity, my closing statement to my audience, regardless of size, became, "I know more women's history than everyone here put together, and I know only very little. Please seek out your history, learn it, love it, embrace it, enjoy it, relish what you have done, who you are, and pass it on."

My online column became my way of giving away women's history and passing it on beyond my limited lecture groups. I could now reach women around the world. But oh, so often I wished I had a book of my columns in my hand, to hand to women in my lectures and in my social network, to give as gifts to family and friends, to give to these women their history that they, too, could have it and give it to others. Thus, began my journey to publish *A Thesaurus of Women from Cherry Blossoms to Cell Phones*.

A Thesaurus of Women is a collection of fifty-two of my online women's history columns. I chose the number fifty-two based on the number of weeks in each year and respectful of most women whose busy multitasking schedules may not provide for time to curl up with a good book. My good book can be read in one sitting, of course, but it also can be picked up and put down repeatedly, let's say fifty-two times, without interruption to story continuity. *A Thesaurus of Women* is written in an easy-to-read, mini-novella style. Each chapter has a beginning, middle, and end. It offers a morning, an afternoon, an evening, or a full year of women's history one week at a time.

I chose the topics for a variety of reasons, many based on the news of the day or personal experiences. "Cherry Blossoms," for example, my very first column, came about after I first saw the blossoms in Washington, DC. Wow! And when I learned they, and the multi-million dollar tourist attraction they are, are there because of a woman who seemed to be overlooked, buried in the blossoms, shall we say, I knew I had to tell of her story.

My columns on the countless women absent in African American history textbooks and passed over and missing in Latino and Native American historic narratives, evolved from my undergraduate courses. Gender disparity proved evident within all cultures across the board, and I became aware of the politics and laws that often define gender disparity and keep it in place. I began to take law courses with a focus on gender, and this aspect is evident in several of my columns.

Some topics came about as a result of my travels to places where I always connected with accomplished women, and/or women's accomplishments. In Hawaii I toured the queen's palace. In Japan I visited the Hiroshima Peace Memorial Park, took part in a traditional tea ceremony with Japanese Association of University Women in Nagoya, and met with Zonta International Women in Tokyo. In Istanbul, where I had to cover to enter the Blue Mosque, and in Seneca Falls, New York, home of the 1848 Women's Convention where I visited the site of the convention and toured the home of Elizabeth Cady-Stanton. I also visited the Sewall-Belmont House Museum in Washington, DC, home and office of Alice Paul, which I encourage you to tour.

My collaborations with the Hull-House Museum in Chicago regarding the annual Jane Addams Day celebrations in Illinois prompted my columns on this remarkable woman and the other remarkable women of Hull House. Those columns citing women's seemingly insatiable quest for peace rather than war, also stemmed from Jane Addams, the first American woman to win the Nobel Peace Prize. The Great Chicago Fire and the great Marshall Field's department store in my great city of Chicago, prompted several columns.

When the financial crisis in 2008 flooded the media, and most eyes were on Wall Street, I cast an eye on the history of women on Wall Street. During that same year, when election of the first female president of the United States almost happened, I glanced around the globe to find other countries where women were or had been president. Then, when it became not this time for the first US female president, another first, appeared, the first FLOTUS of color. I chose to review this unpaid gender specific position and to view several of the previous forty-four white women who served in it.

The unexpected retirement of the first woman on the Supreme Court who was replaced by a man, and then the possibility of another woman or two Supreme Court justices, justified several columns. The fortieth anniversary of the first man on the moon reflected a time when women could not be chosen as astronauts, albeit they were otherwise qualified. The Olympics always offer track records of Olympic women.

I am an amateur astronomer. My interest in physics, astronomy, science in general, how things work, and all things technical, led to those columns on accomplished women in these fields, such as my column on cell phone technology and the beautiful woman who developed wireless communication.

I present my monthly columns as chapters in the chronological order in which they were written. Thus, chapters are not linked to one another and do not appear in any particular order. *A Thesaurus of Women* can be read in sequence or not, as suits your pleasure. And I hope *A Thesaurus of Women* will suit your pleasure.

As I searched for a title to best reflect this treasure of women's history in my anthology, I came upon the tale of how in 1852, Peter Mark Roget had a collection of words he considered to be a treasure and named his collection a thesaurus, the historic *Roget's Thesaurus*. Suddenly, after years of choosing and then discarding several titles that were quite good but never quite right, I knew I had found the title for my book.

A Thesaurus of Women is a treasure of women's rich history that has been all but overlooked, underrepresented, and all but buried women. Today, it is well past any sell-by-date to unearth these earthly women and put them in their deserved place in history without any hesitation or apology.

And so *A Thesaurus of Women* chronicles women (many unknown), their accomplishments (many well known), and the gender obstacles traversed that they could achieve. Each chapter stands alone with the unifying theme of relevant gender facts in all. My writings are intended to enrich women's lives simply by giving women their history that they may take pride in it, thereby pride in themselves. I want every woman to know her history and feel this pride.

For every woman who has crossed over or greatly admired the Brooklyn Bridge, not knowing the civil engineer of that great bridge was a woman, I want her to know that. For every woman who has opened a refrigerator or shopped the frozen food aisle knowing the food inside is safe to eat but not knowing it is so because of a woman, I want her to know that. For every woman who has experienced the beauty of cherry blossoms in Washington, DC, not knowing they are there because of a woman, I want her to know that. For every woman who has a cell phone in her hand or nearby, not knowing it was a woman who first patented this technology, I want her to know that. And I want her to know the role gender played in all of the above as well as in all that is not above but in the pages of *A Thesaurus of Women* as well as in the pages of my next thesaurus of women, already in progress.

As I researched and wrote, I met many women on whose shoulders I now stand, and because of them, I am stronger. I wish this for you, also, that as you read you find a woman, or many women, to whom you can relate and upon whose shoulders you too can stand when you read of her, their, your history.

Your history, *A Thesaurus of Women*, is my gift to you. Embrace it and give it (or a second copy) away that another woman may know her history too. Read, enjoy, and pass it on!

Thank you.

bjz

Introduction

❦

*W*e all marvel at life's treasures. We all take many for granted without even a thought that many are in place because of women. *Who* would have thought?

~~~

Who knew her 1890 environmental plan to plant cherry blossom trees would curb disease as well as beautify the marshlands of Washington, DC, thus lobbied for twenty-four years to convince the district's political powers?

Who wrote a book about a boy wizard named Harry but was identified as the 1998 author with gender-neutral initials because of concern whether boys would buy a book written by a woman?

Who lost her rightful inheritance assets, when, as a widow with no male heirs in 1692, the Salem courts declared her a witch?

Who had her X-ray diffraction photograph depicting the DNA molecule stolen by one of her three male lab mates who, without her, shared the Nobel Prize for their DNA helix model?

Who won two 1964 Olympic gold medals in swimming but was not able to obtain a college athletic scholarship upon her return to the United States because none existed for women?

Who wrote an amendment to criminalize those who denied women their right to vote, not an amendment to grant women a right they always had by virtue of the US Constitution?

Who begged her mother in seventeenth century Mexico to portray her as a boy so she could attend school to study and learn which girls were not allowed to do except in a convent that she entered?

Who had better mathematical skills than her classmate, colleague, and relatively famous scientist-husband who won a Nobel Prize without her?

Who discovered temperatures for packaging and preserving foods to keep them free from contamination, developed refrigerated railroad cars, kitchen and commercial refrigerator-freezers, and designed the egg carton?

Who charted the astronomical skies and calculated star distances that enabled Edwin Hubble and others to make discoveries that dramatically changed our view of the galaxy?

Who accompanied nine teenagers to the entrance blocked by the National Guard and desegregated Little Rock Central High School when escorted in by federal troops in 1957?

Who printed fifty-two thousand flyers the night Rosa Parks was arrested starting the Montgomery bus boycott that desegregated buses all across the South, North, East, and West and ignited the civil rights movement?

Who was jailed and badly beaten for trying to register to vote in Mississippi, barred from the 1964 Democratic National Convention, courageously addressed the credentials committee on national television, and desegregated the 1968 DNC?

Who worked as the virtual "man on the job" of the Brooklyn Bridge construction project but did not have the title of chief engineer?

Who rode naked through her town to get obtrusive taxes on the poor reduced per a challenge from her husband, who had assessed the taxes?

Who developed occupational safety and health standards for others while she worked under unhealthy, gender-abusive standards placed in her path?

Who suffered demands for her resignation as the first female US cabinet member but was the chief architect of the Social Security Act?

Who tested World War II army aircraft for male pilot safety despite women were denied military recognition, pay, uniforms, honors, and burials when they died in action?

Who qualified as America's first astronauts but were not considered for the space program because no qualified woman pilot could be accepted?

Who patented frequency hopping, the basic technology of all wireless communications as in cell phones, but in the 1940s, folks were interested in her beauty not her brain?

She did!

These stories plus more are contained in *A Thesaurus of Women from Cherry Blossoms to Cell Phones*.

Chapter One:
An Ever Blossoming Woman
~

*I*n 1885, pioneering travel journalist Eliza Scidmore wrote of the beautiful cherry blossoms she had seen during an assignment in Japan. She had no idea then of how they would come to define her life and affect the lives of millions worldwide.

Five years later, while home in Washington, DC, Scidmore observed that malaria and yellow fever outbreaks in the Potomac lowlands had become a community health issue. District politicians had long dealt with the ill effects of the DC marshlands. As a form of disease control, army engineers pumped out mud that then created barren land in need of plantings. Scidmore proposed the district plant Japanese cherry blossom trees. Her plan incorporated health, ecological, and aesthetic solutions.

Officials denounced her plan. One cited that a full force of police officers would be needed to keep boys from climbing the trees to pick cherries. Scidmore informed that the trees produced only blossoms, no cherries. Though rebuffed, she did not relent. Convinced her plan would curb disease as well as beautify the district, Scidmore repeatedly presented her proposal for a number of years and personally began raising money to purchase trees she could then donate.

The election of 1908 brought President William Howard Taft and First Lady Helen Herron Taft to the White House. Scidmore knew they had lived in Japan and wrote to the First Lady seeking her support. Mrs. Taft, well aware of Washington's mosquito-infested swamps where tramps gathered and criminals found refuge, was grateful for this opportunity to participate in a much-needed civic improvement, and she promptly responded with her support.

That same spring, Dr. Jokichi Takamine, the Japanese chemist who discovered adrenaline, was in Washington, as was the Japanese consul, Mr. Midzuno. When told of the cherry blossom trees to be planted, they offered First Lady Taft a donation of two thousand trees from Tokyo. The trees arrived in January infested with insects and diseases, and all had to be destroyed. A new shipment of 3,020 healthy trees arrived in 1912. That year, in a simple ceremony attended by only a few, Scidmore watched as Mrs. Taft and Viscountess Chinda, wife of the Japanese ambassador, planted two cherry blossom trees on the northern bank of the Tidal Basin. They were a gift of friendship to the United States from the people of Japan. These two trees still stand marked by bronze plaques that commemorate the occasion but do not commemorate Eliza Scidmore.

In 1934, the first Cherry Blossom Festival was held and in 1940, the first pageant. By 1948, cherry blossom princesses were selected from every state and from them a queen was chosen to reign during the festival. In 1954, a three hundred-year old Japanese Stone Lantern was presented to the United States by the Japanese ambassador to celebrate the one hundredth anniversary of the first peace treaty between these two countries that was signed by Commodore Matthew C. Perry at Yokohama in 1854. Lighting of this lantern officially opens the festival each year.

In 1957, the president of Mikimoto Pearls, Inc. donated to the festival the Mikimoto Pearl Crown of more than two pounds of gold and 1,589 pearls. It crowns the queen each year. In 1958, a Japanese pagoda of rough stone was presented to Washington, DC to symbolize the spirit of friendship between the United States and Japan. In 1965, a Japanese gift of 3,800 cherry blossom trees was given to the beautification program of another first lady, Lady Bird Johnson. In the 1980s, 676 new cherry trees were planted to reinstate the original number of trees.

In 1999, fifty trees bred from the fourteen hundred plus-year-old Usuzumi-zakura cherry tree, a declared national treasure of Japan that grows in Gifu Prefecture, were planted in West Potomac Park. In 2002, sixty-nine trees bred from those of 1912 were planted to ensure genetic tree lineage. Today, the festival, expanded to two weeks, continues to celebrate the friendship between the two countries, and it is a yearly source of millions of tourism dollars that helps the economic welfare of Washington, DC. More than one million visitors were expected in 2006.

The introduction of cherry blossom trees in the nation's capital by Eliza Scidmore, a health and environmental project of unparalleled beauty, created unparalleled wealth of economic, social, and political prosperity and unabashedly created an expression of friendship between two countries that once warred unabashedly. Scidmore, who attended Oberlin College, was a member of the National Geographic Society. She authored seven books plus numerous travel articles.

Eiza Scidmore died in 1928. Her ashes, at the request of the Japanese government, were buried in Japan. This woman who painted pink the red, white, and blue capital of the United States of America is not memorialized in ever-blossoming Washington, DC.

Sources: "She Painted the Town Pink," Sarah Booth Conroy; http://www.washingtonpost.com/wp-srv/local/2000/blossoms0201.htm; http://www.nps.gov/cherry/cherry-blossom-history.htm. September 2003

Chapter Two:
One Woman/Every Baby
~

*A*t a time when few women were allowed to attend, or even attended, college, Virginia Apgar graduated from Mt. Holyoke College with a major in zoology. The year was 1929. Four years later, she received her MD from Columbia University College of Physicians and Surgeons, and she went on to become the most important doctor to every baby born, and still to be born, in a modern hospital worldwide, but I am getting ahead of her story.

Columbia University, founded in 1767, did not admit women until 1917. Apgar was one of the early, if not one of the first females to specialize in surgery. She graduated fourth in her class of sixty-nine men and three other women and won a surgical internship at Columbia Presbyterian Hospital where her surgical skills excelled.

However, when she completed her residency in 1937, women did not do, and were not welcome to do, surgery. After two years devoted to establishing a surgical practice in a chauvinistic culture, it appeared Apgar would not succeed. In unofficial agreement, male physicians limited professional participation of female medical doctors.

Apgar was a single woman, her family was not wealthy, it was the time of the Great Depression, and she needed to support herself. Adhering to gender realities, Dr. Alan Whipple, chair of surgery at Columbia, directed her to practice in anesthesiology, which then was relegated to the domain of nursing, not recognized as a medical specialty, and predominately female.

Apgar entered this emerging field in the first department of anesthesia in the United States at the University of Wisconsin-Madison greeted by ubiquitous gender discrimination. Housing facilities were provided only for men. Women had to seek and secure their own housing. After the program at Madison, she completed a six-month anesthesia internship under Dr. Ernest Rovenstine at Bellevue Hospital in New York.

Dr. Apgar returned to Columbia in 1938 as director of the anesthesia division. She received Board Certification from the American Society of Anesthesiologists in 1939, but encountered a surgical ceiling when soliciting physicians to this new field of medicine. Female anesthesiologists were not accepted as equals by male surgeons and anesthesiology was not respected as an equal specialty. Pay was lower, and well-paid male surgeons, unwilling to "willingly" accept unequal pay for equal work, did not choose to specialize in anesthesiology. Dr. Apgar was the only department member well into the 1940s.

Residency requirements for this newly acknowledged medical specialty was not established until 1946. The division of anesthesia at Columbia did not become a department of research until 1949 when its director, Dr. Apgar, became the first woman appointed a full professor at the Columbia University College of Physicians and Surgeons.

Dr. Apgar's seminal contributions in the development and advancement of anesthesiology are without parallel. Her pioneering contributions in the acceptance of women doctors sliced open the surgical ceiling. However, her foremost medical contribution was for children. Literally every child born in a medical institution since 1949 when defining changes in medicine were taking place all across the United States.

More babies were being born (the baby boomers), and they were being born in hospitals at a greater rate than ever before. As never before, statistics were being recorded producing data that the first twenty-four hours after birth held the highest infant mortality risk.

Previously, newborn babies were considered healthy unless they exhibited a birth defect that was obvious. Now, in a hospital delivery room, the newborn baby was considered a second patient to be evaluated for risk. Intent on the problems of birth defects, Apgar devised a newborn scoring system that measured five vital signs: heart rate, respiratory rate, reflex reaction, muscle tone, and tone of skin color.

In her 1949 study that included 1,760 infants, Apgar collected data that she supported in a 1958 follow-up study of an additional 15,348 infants.

Her findings validated immediate birth diagnoses identifying newborns at risk. This allowed for expeditious treatment in the hospital nursery. Her scoring system became known as the Apgar score, the newborn scoring system at one minute and five minutes after birth that is now common practice.

A ppearance (skin color),

P ulse,

G rimace (reflexes),

A ctivity (muscle activity), and

R espiration (breathing)

The Apgar score has saved countless lives and is considered a standard worldwide. "Every baby born in a modern hospital anywhere in the world is looked at first through the eyes of Virginia Apgar."

In 1974, Dr. Apgar died in her sleep at sixty-five. In 1994, she was pictured on a US postage stamp as part of the Great Americans series, and in 1995 was inducted into the National Women's Hall of Fame in Seneca Falls, New York.

Because she was a woman, Dr. Apgar was unable to be a surgeon, albeit she is unable to be surgically removed from the annals of foremost medical progenitors because she was a woman, discriminatively operational.

Sources: http://www.nlm.nih.gov/changingthefaceofmedicine/physicians /biography_12.html; http://inventors.about.com/gi/dynamic/offsite.htm?site=http://apgar.net /virginia/SELLER%5FPAPER.html; www.greatwomen.org (National Women's Hall of Fame).
October 2003

Chapter Three:
Female & Male Menopause
~

*T*he gains women had made in the paid labor market, because of World War I, immediately began slipping away after the Depression. At that time, gynecologist Robert T. Frank created and linked to women the term premenstrual tension.

Frank, who first published this term in a 1931 article in *The Archives of Neurology and Psychiatry,* wrote that women complained of "a feeling of indescribable tension … unrest, irritability, 'like jumping out of their skin' and a desire to find relief by foolish and ill considered actions."

The fact that these feelings Frank chronicled in women (only in women) who also experienced menstruation made it easy, if not logical, to connect the two and identify hormonal fluctuations as female. Albeit published articles at the time regarding male neurological feelings of tension, irritability, etc., are not found to have received equal, if any, scrutiny.

British physician Katharina Dalton and her colleague Dr. Raymond Greene coined the term premenstrual syndrome in a number of articles published in the 1950s. Dalton titled her 1964 book, *The Premenstrual Syndrome.* PMS, hormones, and hormonal imbalance became synonymous with women, and a vast amount of research studies concerned with female hormones followed.

Once constructed and established as a female menopausal phenomenon, no male menopausal behaviors were questioned to suggest research of hormonal imbalance in midlife men, irrespective that men have hormones and hormonal changes also. Hormonal studies on men did not begin to receive attention until the 1990s.

Psychologist Carol Tavris wrote in 1992 that premenstrual emotional and behavioral symptoms (PMS) "may not have much to do with menstruation and in any case, are not limited to women." Tavris reports that the "evidence of weekday mood cycles in both sexes suggest that treating emotional fluctuations as unhealthy symptoms, and assuming that only women usually manifest them, is misleading ... Men report having as many 'premenstrual symptoms' as women do—when the symptoms aren't called PMS."

Skeptical at first regarding the concept of male menopause, Jed Diamond, in his 1997 book, *Male Menopause,* writes, "After four years of research, I concluded that midlife men have significant hormonal and physiological changes and that 'male menopause' was the proper name to describe what all men experience as they move from the first half of life to the second." Diamond defines it as follows: "Male menopause begins with hormonal, physiological, and chemical changes that occur in all men generally between the ages of forty and fifty-five ... or as late as sixty-five. These changes affect all aspects of a man's life. Male menopause is, thus, a physical condition with psychological, interpersonal, social, and spiritual dimensions."

Many symptoms of male menopause mirror those of the problem that has no name about which Betty Friedan wrote in her 1963 book, *The Feminine Mystique*, i.e., "... the vague emptiness and desolation that plagued many women in the postwar era." It was during the time after World War II when the Rosie the Riveters in the workforce had been displaced as Johnny came marching home and back into the business world where women had had gained autonomy.

Midlife changes in men often occur as their gender-constructed role as provider becomes reconstructed due to emerging new issues such as downsizing, career change, or retirement. Similarly, the hormonal changes of women in menopause occur as their gender-constructed role as mother becomes reconstructed. Women's increased presence in the workforce forces men accustomed to the power and male privilege afforded them by their occupations, to redefine themselves in more humane roles involving home and family.

Simultaneously, traditional gender role-constructs document women's greatest gains on their marital investments occur after about thirty years of marriage. Diamond quotes, "Barbara, a fifty-two-year-old mother of three … 'I can finally begin to think about myself and what I want to do with the rest of my life. For the first time ever, I feel free.'" Willard Gaylin, MD writes, "… the real answer lies not in role reversal but in the gradual mitigation of the sharp distinctions between the two sexes." Nonetheless, in reality it is often difficult to recognize and accept revisions in rigid gender-role constructs.

Diamond writes that there are "similarities in hormonal, physiological, and chemical changes that both men and women experience during this midlife transition." His studies found, and he concluded, that between male and female midlife changes, not only are there similarities, "… there are more similarities than differences." Similarities suggest that women and men may female and male menopause together.

Sources: *Male Menopause*, Jed Diamond; *The Mismeasure of Woman*, Carol Tavris.
November 2003

Chapter Four:
Gender in the Court

~

*I*n his book, *Man & Wife in America,* Hendrik Hartog notes that for more than one hundred sixty years in America, "all the public officials, the authoritative legal voices were all male: judges, legislators, juries."

1692 Salem witch trials: Three-fourths of the accused were women, many who stood to benefit economically from inheritance. They were primarily widows, unmarried women, or married women over forty, unlikely and unable to produce male heirs. Enders A. Robinson (*The Devil Discovered: Salem Witchcraft 1692*) lists the seven male Salem witchcraft trial judges.

1765 British common law: Husband and wife are one person in the law, and that one person is the husband. The wife is *femme covert*–covered woman—she does not exist in the eyes of the law. US law is based in British common law.

1873 *Bradwell v. Illinois*: Myra Bradwell was denied access to the Illinois State Bar because she was a married woman. "Mr." Justice Miller delivered the opinion of the court.

1875 *Minor v. Happerstett*: Dismissed out-of-hand the claim that women had a constitutional right to vote. Virginia Minor was not allowed to register to vote. She and her husband filed suit (as a married woman she could not sue independently). It was a unanimous decision in which "Mr." Chief Justice Morrison R. Waite addressed whether women were even citizens of the United States.

1905 *Lochner v. New York*: Sustained "individual" contract rights to prevail over the rights of the government.

1908 *Muller v. Oregon*: Overturned the Lochner decision, but only for women. "Mr." Justice Brewer delivered the opinion of the court.

1908 Brandeis brief: Written in support of the Muller decision, "Mr." Judge Louis D. Brandeis put forth that legislation designed for women may be sustained even when like legislation is not necessary for men.

1953 *McGuire v. McGuire*: A husband's property rights' case where none of the facts were in dispute. The lower court female judge recognized the traditional wife's right to legal remedy. The Nebraska Supreme Court reversed her ruling. "Mr." Justice Messmore wrote the opinion of the court.

1961 *Hoyt v. Florida*: Upheld the Florida statute that exempted women from jury duty, because they were women with no such exemption for men. "Mr." Justice Harlan delivered the opinion of the court.

1971 *Phillips v. Martin Marietta Corp.*: Marietta refused to hire women for selected positions if they had school-age children, but did not apply this standard to men. Sustained.

1971 *Reed v. Reed*: overturned right of administrator to deceased son's father because he was male. So ruled, despite the parents were divorced, that the son lived with his mother, and did not wish to visit with his father and his new wife. During a court-ordered visit, the son was found dead in the basement of his father's house. Apparently, the boy shot himself with a rifle from his father's gun collection. ACLU attorney Ruth Bader Ginsburg wrote the brief.

1973 *Frontiero v. Richardson*: US Air Force lieutenant could not claim her spouse, a full-time student, as a dependent. Service*men* received dependent benefits automatically. Denied in a lower court, when it reached the US Supreme Court, a young lawyer Ruth Bader Ginsburg wrote for the case, and it won.

1973 *Hodgson v. Robert Hall Clothes, Inc.*: Upheld the district court decision that a wage-gender differential was permissible even though salesmen and saleswomen performed equal work. "Mr." James Hunter, III was the circuit judge.

1974 *Corning Glass Works v. Brennan*: Sustained higher wages to night shift male inspectors than to daytime female employees, even though the law prohibited women from working at night. "Mr." Justice Marshall delivered the opinion of the court.

1976 *Craig v. Boren*: Courts recognized gender as a suspect classification for the first time, but it was a reverse gender discrimination case. Men (Curtis Craig) were unable buy hard liquor under age twenty-one, while women under age twenty-one could. The Supreme Court saw this injustice as gender discrimination and ruled in his favor. "Mr." Judge Brennan delivered the opinion of the court.

1987 *Board of Directors of Rotary International v. Rotary Club of Duarte*: Women were kept out of business clubs, because they were women.

Note: This column is part of an editorial letter (*Daily Herald* 11/15/03) by Barbara Zeitz in response to the article (*Daily Herald* 11/8/03) concerning attorney Joe Rago's reported request to replace a female judge with a male judge, citing a legal concern of gender impartiality toward his male client who was charged with aggravated battery, accused of groping a nurse, and using vulgar language toward her.

Appendix: 2007 *Ledbetter v. Goodyear Tire & Rubber Co.*: Lilly Ledbetter discovered twenty years of gender pay discrimination and filed suit. US Supreme Court upheld gender pay discrimination supporting the 180-day filing limit from the date it began rather than the date discovered. "Mr." Justice Samuel Anthony Alito, Jr. delivered the opinion of the court. February 2004

Chapter Five:
Her Right to Write

~

S ince the beginning of the written word, many literary works by women went unsigned as a way to preserve them, as women's works often were (are) devalued or ignored and destined to obscurity. Virginia Woolf wrote, "For most of history, 'Anonymous' was a woman."

In the early nineteenth century, when it was not considered lady like for a lady to write, publish, and market books, three famous sisters wrote under male pseudonyms to hide their improprieties from their father, an Anglican preacher, and to hide their gender from male publishers who might not print women's writings. Originally published under the names of Currer, Ellis, and Acton Bell, *Jane Eyre, Wuthering Heights,* and *The Tenant of Wildfell Hall,* became known as the classics of Charlotte, Emily, and Anne Brontë.

As one of the late nineteenth century literary elite in New York, Emma Lazarus wrote poetry, novels, and translated German poems of Heinrich Heine. During the 1870s, more than fifty of her poems and translations were published in trendy magazines. She translated classic Hebrew poems, many included in prayer books. However, as a Jewish woman she encountered bias in two worlds.

At nineteen, she sent a copy of her first novel to Ralph Waldo Emerson. He encouraged her to write and mentored her for several years. However, in his anthology entitled *Parnassus,* he included neither her name nor her poems, not even anonymously.

In 1883, funds were needed for the huge pedestal on which the Statue of Liberty, a gift from France sans pedestal, would rest as it stood in New York Harbor to welcome immigrants to the United States. Constance Harrison organized a fund-raising competition to sell poetry and sketches submitted by famous authors. Entrees included Henry Wadsworth Longfellow, Walt

Whitman, and Mark Twain. Harrison invited Lazarus to enter but Lazarus declined stating, "I cannot write verse on order." Harrison, however challenged her to "Think of the Russian refugee," a theme that pervaded Lazarus' works.

Consumed with her vision of the New World as a haven for refugees of the Old World, Lazarus wrote perhaps the greatest testimonial to the American ideal of freedom, "The New Colossus." It sold for $21,500, an inconceivable amount at that time for a short poem. In part it reads:

"Keep, ancient lands, your storied pomp!"
Cries, she
With silent lips,
"Give me your tired, your poor,
Your huddled masses yearning to breathe free,
The wretched refuse of your teeming shore,
Send these, the homeless, tempest-tossed to me:
I lift my lamp beside the golden door."

Poet, James Russell Lowell wrote, "I liked your sonnet about the statue better than I liked the statue itself. But your sonnet gives its subject a *raison d'être*, which it needed as much as it needed a pedestal."

Lazarus died at age thirty-eight. Memorial services were held for her in *all* New York synagogues. Sixteen years hence, in 1903, the landmark with her poem was in place.

Note: (Women's) History Repeats Itself–1998: Concerned whether boys would buy a book written by a woman, it was suggested this author not use "her" name, but her initials that would be gender neutral and/or could be assumed to be a "his" name. Void of a middle name or an initial, she used Kathleen, her grandmother's name, and positioned *K.* between *J.* and Rowling, as the anonymous woman author of *the* Harry Potter books for boys and for girls.

Sources: *Great Jewish Women* by Elinor Slater & Robert Slater; http://www.jwa.org/exhibits/wov/lazarus/el15.html.
April 2004

Chapter Six:
The Rich Witches of Salem
~

*M*artha Stewart's twentieth century treatment by the law, and the press regarding her financial matters, has been likened to a "bitch-hunt." Psychologist Beverly Valtierra says, "Our culture still has a hard time with hard, powerful women. We still live in a patriarchal society where men call all the shots."

In 1692, witchcraft prosecutions exploded in Salem, Massachusetts. Three-fourths of the nearly two hundred people accused were women. When data only on accused married women is considered, an economic pattern emerges that is entwined with inheritance and the transmission, or the aborted transmission, of wealth and property from men to women.

These women were either: (1) daughters of parents who had no sons (or whose sons had died); (2) women in marriages that brought forth only daughters (or in which the sons had died), or (3) women in marriages with no children at all.

Women who did inherit, who could have been economically independent, often were not because they did not receive their inheritance when they were accused of witchcraft in courts of law. They were women accused and tried by court officials who were men.

Anthropologists have long understood that communities define as witches, people whose behavior enacts the things the community most fears. In a patriarchal community, it was easy to condemn those who did not accept their place in it. Available data shows clearly the particular vulnerability of women without brothers or sons. For, even if all the unknown cases involved women from families with male heirs (a highly unlikely possibility) women from families without males to inherit would still form a majority of convicted and executed witches.

What seems especially significant here is that most accused witches whose husbands were still alive, as their counterparts who were widows and spinsters, were more than forty years old, therefore unlikely, if not unable, to produce male heirs. Indeed, the fact that accusations of witchcraft were rarely taken seriously by the community until the accused stopped bearing children, takes on a special meaning when it is juxtaposed with the anomalous position of "women inheriting" or "potentially inheriting women" in New England's social structure.

Few of the women, however, accepted disinheritance with equanimity. Rather, they took their battles to court, casting themselves in the role of public challengers to the system of male inheritance. The rules of inheritance were not always followed. Occasionally, the magistrates allowed the estate to be distributed in a fashion other than stated.

In most instances, the authorities sided with their antagonists—it indicates how reluctant magistrates were to leave property in the control of women—because it shows that the property of convicted witches was liable to seizure even without the benefit of an attainder law.

Looking back over the lives of these many women, most particularly those who did not have brothers or sons to inherit, one can begin to understand the complexity of the economic dimension of New England witchcraft. Only rarely does the actual trial testimony indicate that economic power was even at issue. Nevertheless, it is there, recurring with a telling persistence once we look beyond what was explicitly said about these women as witches.

No matter how deeply entrenched the principle of male inheritance, no matter how carefully written the laws that protected it, it was impossible to ensure that all families had male offspring. The women who stood to benefit from these demographic "accidents" account for most of New England's female witches.

Source: *Women's America: Refocusing the Past*, 4th Ed., Linda K. Kerber and Jane Sherron DeHart, Oxford University Press, 1995, pp 50–64.
May 2004

Chapter Seven:
Women in Protests and Prisons

~

*W*eeks after the Abu Ghraib prison abuses became public in 2004, a news article quoted how "The culture of sadistic and malicious violence that continues to pervade the prison system violates contemporary standards of decency." However, this quote had been stated five years previous Abu Ghraib by Judge William Wayne Justice of the Texas prison system in 1999 when George W. Bush was governor.

In 1830, under President Andrew Jackson, Congress passed the Indian Removal Act. It sanctioned removing the Cherokee nation to Oklahoma, from Tennessee and Georgia where gold had been discovered. The thousand-mile forced march of Native American Indians, Trail of Tears, opened twenty-five million acres to whites. Militia, white men, would typically enter a house and force the family to leave. American mounted soldiers acted as if they were driving cattle. They rode circles around the people, hooting and shouting insults. Cherokee women and children were repeatedly raped. Food intended for the tribe was sold to locals, and living areas along the trail were filled with excrement. American soldiers ordered their captives to perform acts of depravation so disgusting they cannot be told here. One member of the guard would later write, "During the Civil War, I watched as hundreds of men died ... but none of that compares to what we did to the Cherokee Indians."

In 1917, after President Woodrow Wilson refused to meet with suffrage lobbyists, women peacefully protested in front of the White House for passage of the Nineteenth Amendment. In a five-month period, 168 women were imprisoned. Forced to disrobe in front of a company of men, some were tossed headfirst into prison cells and rendered unconscious. Guards terrorized them. They were fed oatmeal and soups filled with worms, insect-ridden starches, vile saltpeter, and rotting horsemeat.

They were placed in solitary confinement, their mail was cut off, and they were forced to perform hard labor. One prisoner was handcuffed to a spot above her cell door all night; some were imprisoned for months. Conditions in the jail leaked out to the press.

Alice Paul launched a hunger strike and was immediately placed in the psychiatric ward. She was force--fed three times a day through a tube in her throat and wakened hourly throughout the night with a flashlight. Thirty women followed her lead and hunger struck as well. "In all my years of criminal practice, I have never seen prisoners so badly treated," said an Illinois senator.

In 1942, ten weeks after the outbreak of war, President Franklin Roosevelt signed Executive Order 9066 that authorized the exclusion of all persons of Japanese descent. People were registered, numbered, tagged, kept under armed guard, and herded into buses or trains and taken to internment camps. Deportees, surrounded by American soldiers carrying rifles with fixed bayonets, were forced to board militarized freighters and made to strip naked. Many, as Yoshiko Uchida, her sister, and her mother had to live in horse stalls that reeked of urine and horse manure. Uchida recalled that in the mess hall, a cook reached in a dishpan full of canned sausages and "dropped two onto my plate with his fingers ... we tried to eat but the food would not go down ... we were constantly hungry."

In 1962, during the civil rights movement, Fannie Lou Hamer and Annelle Ponder were arrested and severely beaten after attending a voter registration training session in Mississippi. From her prison cell, Hamer could hear Ponder screaming as she was beaten. Hamer was made to lie down on a bench. Two black men were ordered to beat her by two white guards. The white guards held guns to make sure they gave her a good whipping. When they lashed her about her legs, her dress started to move up her thighs. As she reached to pull down her dress, one of the guards pulled it over her head. They beat her with leather straps until her thighs were hard. When told to get up, she did not think she could move.

At the 1964 Democratic convention, Hamer described meeting with Hubert Humphrey, who explained that in his heart he really supported their struggle (Blacks), but his chance to be on the ticket with Lyndon Johnson would be jeopardized if the issue reached the floor.

Sources: *Daily Herald* 5/21/04 Sec 1:13, "Echoes of Abu Ghraib in our own prisons?";
HBO "Iron Jawed Angels"; PBS "Not for Ourselves Alone" only what we could carry, Women in the Civil Rights Movement; www.ngeorgia.com/history/cherokeeforts.html.
July 2004

Chapter Eight:
Noble/Not Nobel Scientific Women
~

*E*nrico Fermi won the 1938 Nobel Prize in physics. He was an expert in neutron and nuclear physics but overlooked the phenomenon of neutron-induced fission. A coworker wrote, "The possibility of fission, escaped us." However, it had not escaped another expert, Lise Meitner, a woman who has not received a Nobel Prize.

Meitner produced the evidence for splitting a uranium atom, nuclear fission, in her lab. Meitner named and explained her finding. Her discovery led directly to Fermi who constructed the first self-sustained nuclear chain reaction. Meitner had collaborated with Otto Hahn who published the laboratory results of Meitner's paper without her name and received the 1944 Nobel Prize in chemistry for his research on fission. Meitner never demanded credit.

Chicago Tribune (2/26/03) headline: "Double crossed? Rosalind Franklin never got proper credit for her [1953] revelation that the DNA molecule was a double helix."

Would this happen to a women scientist today? Astrophysicist Margaret Geller replied, "Of course what happened to her could happen today. It remains very difficult for women to obtain recognition for their intellectual achievements in science."

"The best home for a feminist," James Watson wrote in reverence to Franklin and other female colleagues, "is someone else's lab."

Yet without Franklin's research, Watson and Francis Crick would not have made their DNA structure. Her X-ray diffraction pictures of DNA were stolen by her lab mate Maurice Wilkins and shown to Watson and Crick providing essential information for their model. These three men shared the 1962 Nobel Prize.

Honoring the woman behind DNA, the Chicago Medical School became the Rosalind Franklin University of Medicine and Science in 2003. "As 57 percent of med students in the US are women," Dr. Michael Welch, neuroscience researcher, stroke specialist, new president, and CEO said. "The gender issue was important." This is the first medical school named after a woman.

Jocelyn Bell Burnell was first to detect pulsar signals most suggestive of extraterrestrial intelligent origin. In July of 1967, Professor Tony Hewish designed a large, sensitive radio telescope to pick out quasars. His PhD student Burnell had sole responsibility to operate the telescope and analyze the data from four beams that simultaneously scanned the sky. Burnell, who received ninety-six feet of chart paper a day to analyze, wrote:

> After the first few hundred feet of chart analysis, I could recognize scintillating sources, interference, and detected an occasional series of pulses, which seemed suspiciously manmade. After months of analysis of miles of chart paper, Hewish came to observe and measure data. Just before Christmas, I went to see Hewish and walked into a high-level conference meeting about how to present these results. A paper in January announcing the first pulsar was submitted to NATURE. It has been suggested that I should have had a part in the Nobel Prize awarded to Hewish for the discovery of pulsars. I am not myself upset about it after all I am in good company, am I not!

Rear Admiral Dr. Grace Murray Hopper began a pioneering effort of UNIVAC I, the first large-scale electronic digital computer. Admiral Hopper and her team developed the A-O, her first compiler. It translated symbolic mathematical code into machine code to collect and store programming on magnetic tape. Designed to program language, her B-O was used for automatic billing and payroll calculations. She developed an entire programming language using English, despite being told she could not do this, because "computers didn't understand English." As one of two technical advisers, she defined basic COBOL language, which led to international standards for most computer programming languages. Awarded the first ever Computer Science Man-of-the-Year Award (1969) and many others, her four decades of pioneering computer contributions paved the way for modern data processing technology, i.e., all those hanging chads in Florida.

Sources: www.womeninphysics.com, www.bigear.org/vol1no1/burnell.htm; www.cs.yale.edu/homes/tap/Files/hopper-story.html.
October 2004

Chapter Nine:
SportsWOmanship

~

*E*very February in each of the fifty states, the annual National Girls and Women in Sports Day (NGWSD) is celebrated. It is jointly organized by the National Girls and Women in Sports Coalition composed of the seven premiere girls- and women-serving organizations in the United States. They are the American Association of University Women, Girl Scouts of the USA, Girls Incorporated, National Association for Girls and Women in Sport, National Women's Law Center, Women's Sports Foundation, and the YWCA. Collectively, these organizations have been in existence for more than 432 years and have a membership reach of 5.5 million girls and women.

Thousands of sports educators, coaches, athletic directors, recreation directors, association members, sponsors, students, and parents across the country showed their support of 2005's theme, "More Than a Game." Your support of the day one year will increase visibility for female athletes and advance their struggle for equality in sports that, in addition to access to athletic opportunities, provides access to athletic scholarship opportunities for girls.

As of this writing, male athletes receive $133 million more athletic scholarships annually than female athletes do. Donna de Varona, winner of two gold medals in swimming in the 1964 Olympics, was not able to obtain a college swimming scholarship upon her return home because none existed for women. On May 21, 1973, Lynn Genesko, a swimmer, received the first athletic scholarship awarded to a woman, almost one year to the day that Title IX legislation was legislated in 1972.

United States Representative Patsy Mink (D-Hawaii), an AAUW member, coauthored Title IX with United States Representative Edith Green (D-Oregon). The Title IX preamble reads:

No person in the United States shall, on the basis of
sex be excluded from participation in, be denied the
benefits of, or be subjected to discrimination under
any education program or activity receiving federal
financial assistance.

Sports are not mentioned in this legislation. The legal language of Title
IX *is not* about sports. However, sports are the arena where Title IX has
received an exponential amount of scrutiny and publicity, an arena that
embodies an exponential amount of gender disparity.

Title IX *is* about revenues collected from tax dollars of both genders,
and the gender discriminatory judicial manner in which those tax dollars
are allocated in public educational programs for both genders. Without
gender equitable funding allocation, girls and women's tax dollars fund
the exact sports programs that keep them off the playing field. Reversing
this gender injustice is not the intent of Title IX. The intent of this law is
gender justice of allocated federal funds, nothing more.

Before Title IX, one in twenty-seven high school girls participated in
athletics. Now, one in three girls participate. No Title IX law needed to
be legislated on behalf of men and boys to play sports in federally funded
schools. They just did it, and they did it for 155 years prior to Title IX,
since 1817, when sports first appeared in the American educational system
at the male United States Military Academy.

In 1949, Mink applied to thirteen law schools, only one accepted
women. Today, women make up 24 percent of the nation's lawyers
compared to 3 percent in 1971. The total number of female physicians has
more than quadrupled from 9.1 percent in 1975 to 25.2 percent in 2002.
These statistics are reflective in all professions where higher education is
necessary. As Mitzi Witchger, a national authority on Title IX, professes
and to which Martha Burk eluded at Augusta National Golf Club, "Sports
are about so much more than the score."

NGWSD began in 1987 to remember Olympic silver medal volleyball
player Flo Hyman who, while playing in a tournament in Japan, died of
Marfan syndrome. On NGWSD each year, members wear, and encourage

all girls, boys, women, and men to wear, a T-shirt or jersey that identifies a "her" in sports. Wear T's from T-ball to youth soccer to figure skating to hockey to basketball to softball to lacrosse, etc.

Celebrate the participation and accomplishments of female athletes, and *Ladies, Play Ball!*

Sources: http://www.northnet.org/stlawrenceaauw/sportday.htm
Ronald Kotulak, *Chicago Tribune*, 1:14; 1/12/05
February 2005

Chapter Ten:
Celluloid Ladies

~

When movies were just beginning, they were thought to be a new fad, a silly little thing that would soon go away. Serious businessmen and investors did not take this new twentieth century technology seriously. But women did. They found fundamental film opportunities in the early days of Hollywood's moving pictures industry.

Lois Weber was one of the most important silent film directors. In 1915, she was the highest paid director at Universal Studios turning out films dealing with controversial topics as birth control, poverty, and anti-Semitism. But as the industry grew, men moved in and women were moved out. Weber died broke in 1939.

At the age of eight, deserted by her alcoholic father, Mary Pickford became the family breadwinner. She said she was "the father of my family." In 1909, a shrewd veteran at sixteen, when ushered onto her first movie set and offered five dollars a day, she asked for ten dollars and got it. Within a decade she would say, "I can't afford to work for only $10,000 a week."

Pickford became the most powerful woman in Hollywood. In 1919, Charlie Chaplin, Hollywood director D. W. Griffith, Douglas Fairbanks, Sr., and she formed United Artists. She won an Academy Award in 1929, retired from acting in 1933, and three years later, became vice-president of United Artists. Unaware of her significance in movie history, she died a recluse in 1979. Recent revisionist appreciation credits her films as being technically accomplished.

Starting as a script typist at Paramount Studios, Dorothy Arzner worked her way up to film editor, and in 1927, Paramount let Arzner direct. In the 1930s, female stars were everywhere, but there was only one female director, Arzner. She was an innovative director, one of the first to use theme music in films and the first to use overhead microphones. While filming the first sound movie at Paramount, she hung a microphone from a fishing pole over the actors' heads. Her "boom mic" advanced sound recording for talkies. Her techniques became film standards. Between 1927 and 1943, she directed twenty features and launched the careers of Katharine Hepburn, Joan Crawford, and Lucille Ball. "When men do put women in pictures, they make them so darn sappy and weeping all over the place," Arzner lamented. "There should be more of us directing." (*)

Dawn Steel began in merchandising at Paramount in 1978, moved to production, and produced *Flashdance* in 1983. As head of production in 1985, Steel produced *Top Gun, The Accused*, and *Fatal Attraction*. But while in the hospital giving birth to her daughter, she was removed from her job. As president of Columbia Pictures in 1987, she was the first woman to head a major Hollywood studio. During her two-year tenure, Columbia merged with Tri-Star, released *When Harry Met Sally*, and put into production, *Postcards from the Edge, Awakenings*, and the restoring of *Lawrence of Arabia*. Famous in the media for her brash manner, but refusing to be bitter, she recounted her life in her bestseller, breezy, candid memoir, *They Can Kill You But They Can't Eat You,* which was described by Liz Smith as "a practical primer for ambitious women." Steel died of a brain tumor at age fifty-one.

(*) In 2010, Kathryn Bigelow became the first female director to win an Academy Award for her film, *The Hurt Locker*.

Sources: *Scholastic Encyclopedia of Women in the United States,* Sheila Keenan; 100 Most *Important Women of the 20th Century,* Ed. Myrna Blyth; *Unforgettable Women of the Century,* Ed. Eric Levin; "First Female Film Pioneers," Lynne Elber, *Daily Herald* 5/30/00; *Great Jewish Women* by Elinor Slater & Robert Slater.
March 2005

Chapter Eleven:
Black & Bluestockings

*In the first years of the medieval period, education was mainly for the training of priests. Women, unable to hold religious positions of priesthood, were not allowed to be educated. Henry VIII's break with the Roman Catholic Church closed convents in England, which girls had been able to attend and where they could study and learn. In Spain and Italy, women could attend universities, but only when tolerated by men. During the Renaissance, a desire to learn appeared in women, as did an acceleration of witch-hunts of independent women.

In the eighteenth century, literary clubs known as Bluestocking Societies formed in England and America. Women joined in great numbers. The name, synonymous for women with literary or academic interests, became a put-down.

During the Industrial Revolution, women became dependent on marriage for economic survival. Every young girl was carefully trained to be a good wife and mother, to be subordinate to her husband and to males in general. Girls were taught to defer to men. An education might jeopardize a girl's chance to marry. One father wrote to his daughter, "If you happen to have any learning, keep it a profound secret, especially from the men."

In 1821, Emma Willard argued that girls could and should learn equally with boys. Willard opened a secondary education school for girls. She sat in on the exams of boys so she could teach subjects taught only to boys and thought unwise to teach to females, such as math and science.

In 1833, Oberlin College became the first college in the nation to admit women. In 1837, Mount Holyoke Seminary opened as the first women's college. In 1879, a group of women founded Radcliff College to provide women a Harvard education. Harvard, founded in 1636, steadfastly refused to admit women and did not fully do so until 1975.

Educational opportunities for American women expanded rapidly in the late nineteenth and early twentieth centuries. In the professions, however, most women with college degrees discovered barriers. The Association of Collegiate Alumnae formed in 1881 to address this problem. Their first published research study in 1885, responded to a prominent Boston physician's statement that higher education adversely affects the health of women college graduates. In 1921 they united with the Southern Association of University Women to form the American Association of University Women (AAUW).

Ferdinand Lundberg's 1947 publication *Modern Women: The Lost Sex*, sounded a nearly five hundred page alarm warning, "… careers and higher education [would] lead to the 'masculinization of women with enormously dangerous consequences to the home, the children dependent on it, and the ability of the woman, as well as her husband, to obtain sexual gratification.'"

The conclusions put forth were echoed by editors of popular women's magazines in a myriad of articles that trumpeted femininity. The warning seemed heeded. The number of women attending college fell from 47 percent to 35 percent and by 1958, some 60 percent of women left college.

A 1992 AAUW study provided research data from interviews with three thousand boys and girls that revealed classroom-teaching methods that reinforced negative stereotypes of girls and their abilities. The report synthesized more than thirteen hundred published studies that documented historic theories that girls were not receiving the same quality or even quantity of education as boys.

Sources: *Women's Roots: The History of Women,*, June Stephenson, PhD; *The Boundaries of Her Body*, Debran Rowland, Esq.; *Gender Equity or Bust!*, Mary Dee Wenniger.
April 2005

Chapter Twelve:
True to the Corps

*U*biquitous theories that girls in America's educational system were not receiving the same quality or even quantity of education as boys were duly documented by data in the 1992 landmark AAUW study, "How Schools Short Change Girls." Some thirteen years hence, data on boys' behavior in academia began to surface to claim cause for redress. Whether it be timely, timeless, or about time, evidence citing boys behavior, as woven throughout the history of education, is worthy of review.

The sixty-eight clauses of the University of Oxford's 1379 statutes, mention only one woman by name, the Virgin Mary. The fifty-ninth clause states, "All jobs in the college are to be done by men, as far as possible." The exception was that as, even in the fourteenth century, unlikely that a launderer could be found, a servant could deliver the laundry to a laundress, provided she was old and ugly enough to cause no rumor or scandal.

Academically, women have long been placed on the periphery of college education. One of the early ideas had been simply to put women somewhere else. When the first female students were allowed admission to Oberlin College in 1833, they were limited to the "ladies course" mainly, home economic studies to prepare women to be superior homemakers. Men resented the female presence on campus, and women were segregated.

By 1867, twenty-two colleges in the US were coeducational, but the main reason for admitting women was to fill space in classes. The Radcliff women of 1879 had to reach their seats in a heavily curtained back room where Harvard professors taught them by climbing in windows. In 1883, Columbia permitted women to take exams but not classes with men. Gradually women were allowed to study and to instruct.

Virginia Polytechnic Institute admitted five women to its enrollment of 878, forty-nine years after its beginning in 1872. The corps of (male) cadets publicly protested. The 1922 yearbook reads in part, "I'm peeved and I'm mad, I favor Co-ed extradition, the sooner the better, Or we shall let her murder our very tradition." Soon thereafter, a woman received the highest academic honors at commencement. Her achievement received mixed applause that swelled into protest and threatened pandemonium. The college president stood on stage, shook his finger at the male cadets, and accused them of being jealous of the female students. Quiet was restored.

But on campus, cadets continued to battle female students' achievements, sometimes with [male] faculty support. Not allowed to walk where the cadets' barracks were to access the bookstore to get their books, women had to send messengers, often their fathers. When walking where women were permitted to walk, often water came down from open windows, along with [male] voices yelling. Though not allowed in the athletic association, the women formed a basketball team. The few men who attended the games, always rooted for the opposing team.

Granddaughter of a slave and great-granddaughter of a slave owner, Pauli Murray was denied admission to the University of North Carolina Law School in 1938 due to her race. At Howard University Law School, she was the sole female in her class. On her first day in class, one professor remarked that he did not know why women came to law school, but since they were there, the men would have to put up with them. This inspired Murray to be the top student in her class. She was. Murray applied to Harvard Law School for an advanced degree but was denied admission due to her gender.

Police cleared and arrested women protesters at Columbia in 1968. Threatened by the department of Health, Education and Welfare, HEW in 1972, Columbia's first coed class entered in 1983. After years of lower court appeals, the US Supreme Court ruled in 1996 that as a state school, Virginia Military Institute (VMI) *had* to admit women to its corps of cadets. The six years prior, VMI, spent millions to keep out women.

The Washington Post, April 15, 2005, quotes Larry Summers, then president of Harvard, "You know, universities like ours were structured in their basic structure many years ago, and it's probably an exaggeration, but not too much of one, to say that they were designed by men for men."

Sources: *Gender Equity or Bust!* Mary Dee Wenniger; *Women's America: Refocusing the Past,* Linda K. Kerber and Jane Sherron DeHart; *Women and the American Experience,* Nancy Woloch; http://beatl.barnard.columbia. edu/stand_columbia/TimelineWomen.htm.
May 2005

Chapter Thirteen:
Suffrage Denied, Not Won
~

*T*he year 2010 celebrated the ninetieth anniversary of the Nineteenth Amendment not as a legal document by which women *won* the vote, but as a constitutional amendment that prohibits denial of the right to vote because of gender. Prior to 1920, women voted in the states of Washington, California, Oregon, Arizona, Kansas, Nevada, Illinois, Idaho, Utah, Colorado, Montana, Wyoming, New York, Michigan, Oklahoma, North and South Dakota, Nebraska, Rhode Island, Indiana, Iowa, Maine, Minnesota, Missouri, Ohio, Tennessee, Wisconsin, and the territory of Alaska. In 1917, the men and women of Montana elected the first female of Congress, Jeannette Rankin, to the US House of Representatives.

Political efforts that led to the Nineteenth Amendment actually began at the 1848 Woman's Rights Convention in Seneca Falls, New York, when Elizabeth Cady Stanton stood up and read the motion, "Resolved that it is the duty of the women of this country to secure to themselves their sacred right to the elective franchise." Her words gave birth to the Women's Movement in America.

Stanton's words "secure their sacred right" differ from the words "win the right." Susan B. Anthony's rhetoric in the amendment, based on her finding no wording in the Constitution to ban women's suffrage, is written to "secure women's right" to the elective franchise, not to be given it. Nowhere in her amendment does it say women may now have the right to vote or any such redundant statement about women. The Nineteenth Amendment reads:

> *The right of the citizens of the United States to vote*
> *shall not be denied or abridged by the United States*
> *or by any State on account of sex.*

What this amendment does say is that those people (who all seem to be male), who have been obstructing the justice set forth in the Constitution by prohibiting others (who all seem to be female), from voting, no longer can exercise gender discrimination to deny citizens their constitutional right to vote.

Literally, the amendment is not about women, but about men who will no longer be legally supported or ignored by the law when obstructing voting rights. It is an amendment not about enacting the vote for women, but about enacting the law to prohibit the judicial vigilantism of men, who pushed, punched, prohibited, jeered, jailed, and denied citizens their right to vote. No men seem to have been arrested or jailed for obstructing this constitutional right of all citizens.

Written in 1875, and first presented before Congress in 1878, Anthony's amendment was reintroduced in each succeeding Congress for forty-one years. Its passage in 1919 was exactly as Anthony had written it and exactly as Alice Paul, along with fifteen unrelenting women, hungered and hunger-struck for its passage, and exactly seventy-two years after women's suffrage first was presented publicly for political address in Seneca Falls, New York in 1848.

In 1869, Anthony and Cady Stanton formed the National Woman Suffrage Association (NWSA) to secure federal voting rights for women to end federal gender pay discrimination and to oppose the Fifteenth Amendment (which no longer denied the vote because of race, color, or previous condition of servitude, but not gender). Later that year, the American Woman Suffrage Association (AWSA) organized to advocate for women's suffrage but on a state-by-state basis and not for the other gender issues of the NWSA. AWSA also supported the Fifteenth Amendment granting Negro men the vote, albeit it ignored women. In 1890, they merged into the National American Woman Suffrage Association (NAWSA). With the deaths of Elizabeth Cady Stanton in 1902 and Susan B. Anthony in 1906, zest for the long and laborious work of suffrage faltered in the NAWSA.

In 1913, a zestful, ardent Alice Paul and Lucy Burns proposed an auxiliary to the NAWSA for the sole purpose of passage of a federal amendment. NAWSA reluctantly granted their proposal. Years of peacefully planned parades and protests followed nationwide. In 1916, NAWSA endorsed Paul's plan to get a federal amendment passed and ratified.

In 1917, the United States entered World War I. NAWSA suspended their suffrage advocacy in support of President Woodrow Wilson's decision to enter the war to fight for democracy, despite that for years Wilson had adamantly refused to support women's suffrage. Paul, however, adamant in her pursuit of a federal amendment seeking democracy at home for women, refused to suspend her suffrage advocacy during yet another war (it had been suspended fifty-two years prior during the Civil War). NAWSA withdrew its support from Paul and literally shut down her auxiliary.

Paul formed the National Woman's Party (NWP) in direct response to Wilson's refusal to support women's democracy while fighting for German democracy. Paul began small groups of peaceful protests for women's equal suffrage directed directly at Wilson, directly in front of the White House. Protests continued for fourteen months, when subsequently 168 women were arrested and literally thrown into jail. They were forced to disrobe before men, placed in solitary confinement, fed rotten food, forced to do hard labor, and more.

News of their inhumane treatment filled the newspapers nationally and worldwide. Outrage in America stirred up support for the women and their suffrage struggle. NAWSA, backed by twenty-eight states with sanctioned women voters, withdrew its support of Wilson. Wilson, who planned to run for reelection in 1920, needed women's votes.

In 1918, Wilson addressed Congress to support the women's suffrage amendment. In 1919, the amendment was passed in the House on May 21, in the Senate on June 4, and ratified in Tennessee on August 26, 1920. Thus, this summer and every summer on Women's Equality Day—August 26:

> *Celebrate the 19th Amendment for what it truly is,*
> *A law, which confirms that she too had the vote,*
> *Which all along he proclaimed … was just his.*
> *The law, as you see, does not say that she "won,"*
> *A right she already possessed.*

The law simply states, her right can't be denied,
Regardless of what "he" professed.

Sources: "Iron Jawed Angels," HBO Video, 2004; http://www.essortment.com/womens-suffrage-movement-united-states-32594.html; http://en.wikipedia.org/wiki/Women%27s_suffrage_in_the_United_States; http://www.suite101.com/content/woodrow-wilson-and-the-19th-amendment-a192861.
July 2005

Chapter Fourteen:
The Supremes

~

*C*omposition of the Supreme Court is stated in the US Constitution that was defined and signed by the thirty-nine men who convened in Philadelphia in 1787. Their Constitution is a living document that is interpreted by judges in our courts, often with decisions that traverse, decisions that govern both men and women.

In the 1930s, Chief Justice Hughes stated, "We are under a Constitution but the Constitution is what the Judges say it is." The Supreme Court is the highest court from which there is no appeal. Its decisions are the law of the land. Higher court judges can overrule lower court judges. And lower court judges have a greater propensity to be women.

In 1981, Sandra Day O'Connor became the first woman appointed to the Supreme Court by the first man, of the forty-two men to the date of this column, who appointed 106 men and two women Supremes. After 192 years of law making-and-breaking decisions, O'Connor was the first woman afforded the opportunity by the first male president to speak from the highest court of the land on decisions that legally bind both men and women.

O'Connor evaluated each case on a case-by-case merit basis. Rather than being strictly liberal or strictly conservative, she was both and neither, often the swing vote. When the Supreme Court heard oral arguments about a widow denied use of her property, most of the justices focused on legal precedents. Justice O'Connor said, "Why not give this poor, elderly woman the right to go to court?" In a student-on-student case of a fifth grade girl sexually harassed by a boy, O'Connor rejected the argument that this decision would teach "little Johnny" the wrong lesson about federalism. Instead, she argued, it would ensure that "little Mary may attend class."

Ruth Bader Ginsburg's most famous case to date, prior to her Supreme Court appointment in 1992, may be the 1991 decision to allow women to attend the all male Virginia Military Institute (VMI). Attorney Ginsburg reformulated the question before the court to be, not whether a female can be admitted to the all-male VMI, but whether the government can constitutionally deny admittance to a qualified applicant because of gender.

Her philosophy of equal treatment for men and women who do not conform to society's gender-based stereotypes, allows men to assume traditional female roles. (i.e., her victory in the case of a young widower whose wife had died in childbirth and because of his gender was ineligible to receive Social Security benefits enabling him to work part-time and stay home to care for his baby.)

An all-male, liberal Supreme Court affirmed *Roe v. Wade* in 1973. In the 1992 challenge to *Roe*, O'Connor's swing vote upheld it. In 1993, Ginsburg openly criticized the court's opinion, stating that had the Supreme Court struck down *Roe*, the process of legislative liberalization might have continued gradually throughout the states, without the political divisions engendered by *Roe*. Ginsburg dissented with the ruling that halted the 2000 presidential ballot counting in Florida, O'Connor voted with the majority.

Appointing a woman to replace O'Connor may or may not ensure *Roe*. But with a man appointed and confirmed to fill this woman's place, the opportunities to speak on law-of-the-land decisions that legally befall both men and women, will be spoken by eight men and one woman Supremes.

Source: *Chicago Tribune*, 8/18/97.
September 2005

Chapter Fifteen:
Poetic Relativity

~

As a female intellectual, she was a rare phenomenon in seventeenth century Hispanic society. Obsessed to study, she learned to read at age three, to write at age five, learned Latin in less than twenty lessons, and begged her mother to dress her as a boy that she could attend the university in Mexico City. But this was impossible.

Sor Juana Ines de la Cruz is considered to be the first North American feminist. All her written works are in defense of women's intellectual rights. Recognized as a poet of the first magnitude in Hispanic literature, her poetry expresses her interest in science, astronomy, mathematics, philosophy, physics, and in them all, gender equity. The *Dream* is considered her most important work, but her most famous poem begins:

> *Hombres necios que acusáis*
> *(Stupid men who accuse)*

As a playwright and author, the *Repuesta* is her preeminent prose work. Sor Juana expresses her rebellion against a world based on man's superiority to women by asserting her belief in the absolute equality between the sexes and in the right of a woman to intellectual activity in an autobiographical letter. Alberto G. Salceda calls it the Magna Carta of intellectual freedom for women in the Americas. It is speculated she would have been a scientist had the time and place allowed. The Mexican Fine Arts Museum in Chicago (the finest in the country) holds a festival in her honor every fall.

Mileva Maric and Albert Einstein were university classmates. Mileva was always at the top of her class with her highest grades in math and physics. Her interest in math was said to be insatiable. Albert, awkward in math, tracked her down to be his study mate. Their goal was the mathematization and unification of physics. Young and in love, he wrote to her, "How happy and proud I will be when we two together have victoriously led our work on relative motion to an end!"

In 1905, during their married years, several articles attributed to Albert, one on the "principle of relativity," appeared in a German physics journal. The original submission was signed "Einstein-Marity." Marity (Maric) was the maiden name of Mileva. Serbian women had little chance in those days other than as wives attached to their husbands. Mileva is alleged to have said, "We are both one stone." She perhaps hoped that one day he might acknowledge her work. However, Albert, a misogynist, degraded her in letters, ended their marriage, and gave up their children. Undisputedly, his years married to Mileva were his most productive. In 1964, the Regional Cultural Association in Switzerland declared the Einstein house a cultural monument. A plaque placed at the entrance reads:

> *In this house lived Albert Einstein,*
> *the creator of the relativity theory,*
> *and his scientific assistant and wife,*
> *Mileva.*

Sources: Georgina Sabat-Rivers in *Latin American Writers*, Carlos A. Solé, Ed.; *Albert Einstein: The Incorrigible Plagiarist*, Christopher Jon Bjerknes; *In Albert's Shadow: The Life and Letters of Mileva*, Milan Popovic; *Einstein's Daughter*, Michele Zackheim; *Einstein in Love*, Dennis Overbye. October 2005

Chapter Sixteen:
Business Women of Fashion
~

For many nineteenth century New England young women in farm families, dressmaking and millinery work offered opportunity for independence and creativity, as they were acceptable enterprises for women. Fashion directed businesses that catered to a female clientele, separate from the mainstream industries run by and for men, were the backbone of the female economy.

In the mid-1800s, Ellen Demorest built a business for women who wished to appear fashionable in public. It grew from a millinery shop in upstate New York to a fashion industry in New York City where Brooks Brothers and Lord & Taylor had opened shops. Her husband published a women's fashion magazine and developed a pattern-selling business. Their fashion empire followed their social principles with a special interest in improving the lives of women.

African-American women, treated as equals with whites, worked at comparable pay and were invited to company social events. When wealthy, influential customers objected, they were invited to shop elsewhere. Once deemed an exclusive luxury for the wealthy, Demorest linked fashion with needy women giving them an acceptable way to achieve economic autonomy. A New York City reporter said, "No woman has done more than Mme. Demorest to secure the best interests of her sex."

A Jewish immigrant alone in New York in 1895, Lena Himmelstein quit her job as a seamstress to marry David Bryant. Sixteen months later, now a destitute widow with an infant son, she began a seamstress business in her Manhattan apartment. Her dress design for an expectant mother began a fashion venture aimed at equality and freedom for pregnant women doomed to housebound seclusion once they could not conceal their "condition."

Her bold fashion statement challenged the tradition of secrecy and shame placed on pregnant women and brought maternity wear and pregnant women out of the closet, so to speak. Though the *New York Herald* hesitantly ran her first advertisement, expectant mothers did not hesitate to shop, and they bought out the store in one day. Later, her introductory designs for the full-figured woman addressed women ignored by the fashion industry. For the first time, full-figured women could buy fashionable clothes. Sales in her plus-size clothing line soon overtook the maternity line.

When opening a bank account, a teller misread her signature, and Lena who was too insecure to correct him, accepted his error and her new name of Lane. In 1917, Lane Bryant reported yearly sales of one million and five million in 1923, but she never forgot her poor beginnings. She offered employee benefits long before company plans were common. She promised a free wardrobe to any woman whose wardrobe was destroyed in a disaster, and during World War II, her stores were centers for clothing donated to war victims.

Ida Rosenthal, a young Jewish immigrant from Russia, remodeled the fashion industry from inside and out. While the 1920s flapper dress looked best on women with flat chests, full-breasted, fashion-conscious women wore a bandage-like undergarment to reshape their bodies. "Nature made women with a bosom," Rosenthal commented, "so why fight nature?" She redesigned the undergarment as two cups joined by elastic and called it the Maiden Form Brassiere. In business with her husband, they introduced the first nursing bra, the first full-figure bra, and what came to be the standardized A, B, C, and D-cup sizes.

Source: *Enterprising Women: 250 Years of American Business,* Virginia G. Drachman.
November 2005

Chapter Seventeen:
The Ice Lady Came

~

*T*he food in the freezer, the freezer in the refrigerator, the refrigerator itself, the frozen food aisles in modern grocery stores, railroad and truck freezer cars, the ice cream pushcart, etc., all use food preservation health standards, as we know them, thanks to Mary Engle Pennington. As a female bacteriological chemist at the turn of the twentieth century, Pennington developed methods of handling, packaging, and preserving foods, because as people moved to cities, fruits and vegetables formerly picked from backyard gardens now needed to be shipped long distances. Food contamination was a major health issue, mainly due to unsanitary handling procedures and to spoilage from unseen bacterial growth.

Pennington's work was devoted to keeping foods fresh and safe to eat from the farm to the city. She researched cooling temperatures that would prevent bacterial growth and preserve food quality. She created scientific standards for food storage and transportation of perishables, especially milk, poultry, eggs, and fish, but most importantly, ice cream. She designed refrigerated railroad cars and freezers, as well as refrigerator-freezers for the home. Today's commercial refrigerated and frozen food sections are a direct result of her innovations. The egg carton is her design.

At the age of twelve, Pennington had found a chemistry book at her library. The book introduced her to the unseen world of atoms and molecules in which we live. She was instantly fascinated and hooked on this invisible world. At eighteen, she entered the University of Pennsylvania where she completed the requirements for a bachelor degree of science. However, the university did not grant degrees to women. Instead, for her academic studies, she was awarded a "certificate of proficiency." She was encouraged by some of her professors to stay at the University of

Pennsylvania where she eventually earned and was awarded her PhD. She then did postdoctoral research at Yale.

Recruited by the US Department of Agriculture (USDA) in 1905, Pennington worked for the passage of the first 1906 Pure Food and Drug Act, which led to the formation of the Food and Drug Administration (FDA). In 1908, she became Chief of the Food Research Lab for the FDA.

In 1919, President Hoover awarded her the Notable Service Medal. The American Society of Heating, Refrigeration, and Air-Conditioning Engineers recognized her in 1923 as the foremost American authority on home refrigeration. She received the Garvan Medal in 1940, and in 1947, was elected fellow by the American Society of Refrigerating Engineers. In 1959, she was the first woman elected to the Poultry Historical Society Hall of Fame. In a ceremony I was privileged to attend in 2002, Mary Engle Pennington was inducted into the National Women's Hall of Fame at Seneca Falls, New York.

Sources: National Women's Hall of Fame (www.greatwomen.org); Journal of Chemical Education; Women in Chemistry; http://chemheritage.org/women_chemistry/food/pennington.html.
March 2006

Chapter Eighteen:
Of Sweatshops Past and Present
~

*T*he clothing industry has always been, and continues to be, a place where poor women could find work. At the turn of the twentieth century, New York City was an entry port to millions of poor immigrant workers. Eighty percent of the garment shop workers were women, and of these 70 percent were between the ages of sixteen and twenty-five who could not speak English. Most were of Italian, Polish, Russian, Hungarian, German, or Jewish descent.

Working conditions were unsafe and unsanitary. Workdays were long. Wages were low. Work was monotonous. Talking was not allowed. Sexual malevolence domineered. When male bosses paid the women, mistakes in shorting their pay were common. Scared of losing their jobs, women who knew they had sewn ten or fifteen more pieces for which they were not paid, could not object. Factories were rarely inspected for safety and fire laws were lax.

The Triangle Shirtwaist Factory occupied the top three floors of a ten-story wooden building in New York City. The building had two elevators and two narrow escape staircases, one with a door kept locked. Doors on each floor were kept locked to keep workers in, as well as to prevent employee theft. Sewing machines were crowded close together. Aisles to fire escapes were blocked or nonexistent.

On March 25, 1911, a fire broke out. Workers were trapped behind the locked doors. Within minutes, 140 of some 600 workers, mostly young women, were dead. Many jumped down elevator shafts or out of windows. Burned bodies lay dead across sewing machines.

The building was up-to-date for the time and said to be fireproof. What burned so quickly was the fabric of the shirtwaists that hung on lines immediately above the heads of the women, as well as the trimmings and cuttings immediately below them, strewn about their feet on the floor. It was not the first time women burned alive while at work. But with so many for so few jobs, it mattered little. It had been stated that the fire was started for insurance purposes.

The owners, Black and Harris, were tried on manslaughter charges. The two men testified that the door to the fire escape was open, but according to the workers, it was never unlocked. The jury of men, who decided whether the owners knew that the doors were locked at the time of the fire, acquitted the owners of any wrongdoing.

The Women's Trade Union League led a campaign to probe working conditions. In response, the governor of New York State appointed an investigating commission. Important factory-safety legislation followed. Frances Perkins, executive secretary of the New York Committee on Safety, who had watched the building burn, assisted in the investigation and become a lifelong advocate for workers. Perkins later served as Secretary of Labor under President Franklin Delano Roosevelt. Sweatshops Present continue to be a place where poor women ...

Note: The tragic Triangle Shirtwaist Factory fire became the cause *célèbre* of International Women's Day celebrated around the globe each year on March 8.

Sources: *1001 Things Everyone Should Know About Women's History*, Constance Jones; *A History of Women in America*, Carol Hymowitz and Michaele Weissman; *Women's America*, Linda K. Kerber and Jane Sherron DeHart; http://www.ilr.cornell.edu/trianglefire/narrative6.html; http://www.csun.edu/~ghy7463/mw2.html.
April 2006

Chapter Nineteen:
Three Mary's Magdalene
~

*I*n a 591 Easter sermon, Pope Gregory the Great conflated Mary of Bethany who anointed Jesus' feet and wiped them with her hair; a repentant sinner who also anointed and was forgiven by Jesus; and Mary of Magdala, henceforth to be remembered as a prostitute.

In Luke 8, Mary Magdalene is an independent woman traveling with Jesus and two other women. They are to have been restored to health by Jesus who cast seven demons from Mary Magdalene. This may imply the women faced social, mental, or spiritual issues, which Jesus helped them address. "Possessed by demons," did not necessarily make Mary Magdalene a sinner. The Bible references those with mental or physical illness as having demons.

Mary's lifestyle and economic means may indicate she is widowed, divorced, or perhaps a self-sufficient woman living independently. She is written as a "strong woman," present at the crucifixion and the tomb of Jesus. In some accounts, the male disciples ran away when Jesus was crucified. Peter cowardly denied Jesus three times. Mary Magdalene stood strong at the cross.

Most significant about Mary Magdalene is that she is a beloved disciple of Jesus. The "First Apocalypse of James" claims Jesus had twelve male and seven female disciples, and Mary is mentioned by name. Scholars agree little was written about Mary, because she was a woman.

Karen King, a historian of early Christianity at the Harvard Divinity School, argues that Magdalene was misrepresented as a prostitute to undermine her authority as a church leader. Reverend Pamela Giese, a Gnostic priest at the Church of the Four Holy Crown Martyrs in Villa Park, Illinois, notes the strain between Peter and Mary in the Gnostic gospels. She offers how Peter is portrayed as an angry man, and that it was Mary whom Jesus cited as the rock on which to build his church. Marvin Meyer, one of the foremost scholars on Gnosticism, notes that parallel stories in Luke convey a picture of a world divided by gender. Reverend Giese, on the confusion of the three women, told her mother that a lot of history of women in the church had been repressed. Her mother responded, "Pammy, everybody knows that."

The gospels of Matthew, Mark, Luke, and John, appear in the Bible as the chosen four of many gospels. The thirteen papyrus books bound in leather and discovered in Egypt in 1945, the Gnostic gospels, prove to be Coptic translations of ancient gospels other than those in the Bible.

Princeton Professor Elaine Pagels of the Harvard doctoral program of the history of Christianity notes the feminine element of the divine in these Gnostic gospels and suggest women shared with men in positions of authority. The disciples were male and female. God was celebrated as Father and Mother. And, they suggest a superior feminine power.

The term prostitute, by which Pope Gregory identified Mary Magdalene in the late sixth century stuck, or was deliberately advanced. Whether a prostitute meant a woman supporting herself or a prostitute as we define the word today, scholarship lacks to identify Mary Magdalene with the unnamed woman in Mark, or with Mary of Bethany, sister of Lazarus in Luke and John.

Sources: *The Five Books of Moses,* Robert Alter; *Gnostic Gospels* and *The Secret Gospel of Thomas,* Elaine Pagels; *The Gospels of Mary,* Marvin Meyer. May 2006

Chapter Twenty:
Colossal Women in Publishing
~

Thirty-nine men, whose names are duly chronicled and historically known, designed and signed the Declaration of Independence. The publisher, whose name is not so duly chronicled or historically known was declaredly a woman to note.

In Colonial America, (Mary) Katherine Goddard was a distinguished publisher, a position that did not come easily to her because of her gender. When she was nineteen, the oldest of four children in a prominent family, her father, a doctor, and the postmaster of New London, Connecticut, died.

Katherine watched as her younger brother William was designated head of the family. He was given substantial inheritance funds with which to start a business. In the eighteenth century (1757), this was the typical patriarchal pattern of passing down family wealth.

The inheritance enabled William to leave New London for Providence, Rhode Island, where he established the first newspaper there, the *Providence Gazette*. Though their mother Sarah Goddard adhered to the gender protocol of the day by fostering her son, she also fostered her daughter in this new family business when she moved with Katherine to Providence to help William. His *Gazette* had very few subscribers.

Three years after they arrived, William left for greater publishing opportunities in New York and Philadelphia. Katherine and Sarah stayed on and continued to publish the *Gazette*. They opened a bookshop and added a bindery to their growing enterprise. Three years later, they sold their businesses to help William in Philadelphia with his grander printing pursuits, which included founding the *Pennsylvania Chronicle*. Two years later when Sarah died, Katherine continued on her own to manage and publish the *Chronicle*.

In 1773, William repeated his seemingly insatiable quest for bigger and better and moved to Baltimore to start that city's first newspaper, the *Maryland Journal*. While in Baltimore, he became deeply invested in establishing a national postal system. Once again, Katherine followed to help her brother publish, but she would no longer accept taking control under the banner of his name. The official masthead of the *Journal* credited the rightful publisher and read, "Published by M. K. Goddard."

Katherine published the *Journal*, owned and operated her bindery and bookshop, and was appointed to manage the Baltimore post office. Thus, she became the first woman postmaster in the colonies. Her reputation, her political involvement, and her publishing skills were adroit.

When the Declaration of Independence was to be published, Katherine was chosen by the Continental Congress of 1777 to print it. At the very bottom of this first official United States document that did not mention the rights of women, she documented that it was: Printed by Mary Katherine Goddard.

Note: (Women's) History Repeats Itself: In the twentieth century (1948), through the typical patriarchal pattern of passing down family wealth, thousands of shares of *Washington Post* stock was transferred to Phil and Katharine Graham by Katharine's father who owned the *Post*. Phil was given the larger number of shares because, according to Katharine's father, no man should be in the position of working for his wife. Katharine writes of how, at the time, she not only concurred, but also was in complete accord. After Phil's ruinous years and ultimate suicide in 1965, the floundering *Washington Post* flourished when: Published by Katharine Graham.

Sources: *Enterprising Women: 250 Years of American Business,* Virginia G. Drachman; *Personal History,* Katharine Graham.
July 2006

Chapter Twenty-one:
Field's Ladies Macy
~

When the American Civil War ended in 1865, Marshall Field and Levi Leiter opened a store on the corner of Washington and State streets in Chicago. Their marble-fronted palace catered to women.

The Great Chicago Fire of 1871 destroyed the building; intense heat pulverized the marble. Field had salvaged much merchandise and opened a temporary store in a horse barn at State and Twentieth. Though not elegant, elegance prevailed. Red velvet draperies wrapped pillars and distinctive carpets adorned walls. Marshall Field greeted every lady at the door, salesmen were distinctively dressed, and flowers garnished department heads' lapels.

In 1873, the store returned to Washington and State in a new, five-story mansard-roof building with a huge glass dome in its center. Glowing gas chandeliers hung from frescoed ceilings. Clerks were patient, polite, and persistently reminded customers that for a full refund, goods could be exchanged or returned. The "Customer is always right" was drilled into Field's salesclerks. If he saw a customer arguing about a purchase, he would gently pull on the clerk's coattail and whisper to him, "Give the lady what she wants."

The typically low wages of working women forced many women to work nights to supply the male demand for escorts and prostitutes. Store workers at Field's, however, had glamour jobs midst ladies they wished they were.

The elite society that emerged after the Great Fire produced a "New Chicago Woman" who set fashion trends and shopped at Field & Leiter's. The business of shopping was an accepted activity for women of that era. It grew to be a liberating escape for middle- and upper-class women who were locked into Victorian traditions and homes.

Shopping became a form of urban entertainment—window-shopping, a new urban pastime. City stores catered to women and recognized their new marketplace buying power. An estimated 99 percent of State Street purchases were women transacted.

Field bought out Leiter in 1880, and by the turn of the century, Marshall Field's was the largest retail store on earth. When told that women were leaving his store to go home for lunch, he opened a small tearoom and a floor of elegant restaurants resulted.

In the male-dominated culture, most professions and all professional clubs were closed to women. The Union League Club of Chicago with its deep leather chairs, fireplaces, newspapers, and stewards who would quickly fetch beverages or edibles, was a bastion sans women, as was the Dearborn Club, the Rotary, and other male organizations. Membership was limited to professional and business*men* of high ranking.

Field's became a woman's world analogous to a men's club. At Marshall Field's, a woman could socialize, eat in restaurants, lounge in parlors, try on clothes, order deliveries, and return any merchandise that failed to please. She could execute her day amid objects of beauty and value from around the world. Attentive clerks showered shoppers with personal courtesies in an unhurried manner. Customers were not negotiated with, but waited upon. Rich or poor, famous or not, every woman was treated honorably. No one was to leave Field's store dissatisfied.

Marshall Field left his store and the world on January 16, 1906. A bell rang, shades were drawn, aisles darkened and the business was suspended in his hallowed monument. After five days, the new president, John G. Shedd, reopened and activated plans to tear down the building and build anew.

On September 30, 1907, some eight thousand people, mostly women, waited outside under a prominently hung clock for 8:00 a.m. and the doors to open. Stepping inside, they were awed by the Tiffany dome six floors above and all the grandeur beneath.

Rumors suggested Shedd might add his name to the store, but he retained the Marshall Field name. When Shedd retired in 1923 to build an aquarium, the new managers also saw to retain the Marshall Field name well. Macy's, Inc. chose to acquire the Marshall Field flagship department store in 2005 and in September 2006 officially chose not to retain the name, as Field's ladies Macy.

Sources: *Give The Lady What She Wants,* Lloyd Wendt and Herman Kogan; *City of the Century,* Donald L. Miller; *Chicago,* Finis Farr.
September 2006

Chapter Twenty-two:
Mrs. O'Leary Cowed

~

*E*XTRA! EXTRA! Read All About the Great Chicago Fire! More than six hundred fires blazed in Chicago between 1870 and 1871, some quite "great," and of those fires, around twenty-seven occurred during the first week of October 1871. Months of drought had seen only four inches of rain and none the weeks prior to October 8. A city ordinance forbade the use of open flame candles or lamps where hay or straw was stored. Nevertheless, most fires began in barns.

A "great" fire near Patrick and Catherine O'Leary's property the night of October 7 had burned most buildings to the ground in a five-block area. Roughly, half of Chicago's firefighters fought this Saturday night fire well into the night and the next morning. Generally, it was typical to conclude such "great" fires with a good drunk. Fatigued firefighters, lacking a night's sleep, were unprepared for the immediate infamous fire that followed.

Catherine O'Leary owned five cows and ran a business selling milk. Rumor, which quickly turned into gospel, set forth that Mrs. O'Leary's cow started the Chicago fire by kicking a lighted lantern in the O'Leary barn. But that night, the O'Leary's had retired early. Their neighbors held an Irish party and one man, Peg Leg Sullivan, had lingered outside to listen to the fiddle music. He noticed the fire, pointed out the fire's location, and yelled the "Fire!" alert.

The firehouse watchman on duty ordered the fire alarm operator, William Brown, to sound the alarm for Box 342, which was an incorrect address. Aware of his error, the watchman ordered Brown to sound a corrected alarm, but Brown decided that would cause confusion to firefighters already rushing in the wrong direction. Brown's decision could well be the cause of the city's immense destruction.

Prompt response was credited for success in putting out the other six hundred fires before they spread out of control. The spread of flames, starting in O'Leary's barn or not, could definitely have been contained had the response been correct and prompt. Brown was not cited for his conduct during Chicago's destruction and seemingly was not even questioned, though sightseers and reporters with questions swarmed the site of the O'Leary barn for weeks.

Newspaper accounts of investigations regarding the causes circulated, and a photo of the O'Leary house untouched by the fire was printed. Reportedly, no one interviewed Brown, Sullivan, or Mrs. O'Leary, who had made a sworn statement supported by affidavits denying the charges. An official inquiry did verify that Mrs. O'Leary, her husband, and their three children were in bed when the flames first burst.

The rumor was never substantiated by fact, and news spread throughout the world of an uncontrolled fire.

As years passed, the press and meddlesome spectators continued to torment Mrs. O'Leary. She and her family eventually moved away from their home. Still, each year until her death and on the anniversary of the fire, reporters would besiege her home and attempt to get a statement from her. Though she never agreed to speak with them or permit herself to be photographed, bogus interviews and pictures of her milking the supposed cow appeared in numerous publications. Some wrote she was an Irish drunk who started the fire because she was taken off welfare, a program she never was on. As the written abuse of her prevailed, Mrs. O'Leary became a virtual recluse. She died in shame in 1895.

In 1900, Michael Ahern confessed that he and two male co-reporters, James Haynie and John English, had concocted the "cow-kicking-over-the-lantern" hypothesis during their investigative reporting after they had seen a broken kerosene lamp in the O'Leary barn.

In 1997, a resolution of the Chicago City Council acquitted Mrs. O'Leary and her cow from the cause of the Great Chicago Fire. Neither the men responsible nor the reporters, who altered the news, have been duly accused—yet. But accusations can loom until the cows come home.

Sources: *The Great Fire: Chicago 1871*, Herman Kogan and Robert Cromie; *Smoldering City*, Karen Sawislak; *Chicago and the Great Conflagration*, Elias Colbert and Everett Chamberlin; *City of the Century*, Donald L. Miller.
October 2006

Chapter Twenty-three:
Queen for a Dole
~

*H*awaii's last monarch, Queen Liliuokalani, was dethroned and imprisoned in 1893 when US Marines were ordered to defend by military force the American pineapple and sugar interests in her Hawaii. In the year of her death in 1917, Liliuokalani asked that her story be told because "the same betrayal of all peoples can happen if they do not understand."

When missionaries arrived in 1838, Hawaii was a matriarchal society, spiritual, and interlocked with nature, where there was life and there were gods. Perceived as savage, sermons of a vengeful Calvinistic God were preached to them in New England style churches by missionaries who did not understand many values, that is, the *aloha* and the *hanai*.

Hawaiian self-worth faltered. Some worked for *haole* (foreign) businessmen and many women became *haole* domestic servants. As missionary laws grew dominant, *haole* promised to put natives in authority when they were deemed ready to hold political power.

In 1863, King Kamehameha IV died of grief. Many Hawaiians believed he no longer could cope with the *haole* world. Dedicated to Hawaiian policies, he refused to sign the 1852 Constitution, fearing his people were not ready for a democracy designed for and by Americans. History verifies Hawaiians' proclivity for *aloha* and *mana*, (guidance and leadership) from their kings. Mark Twain noted Hawaiians loved their chiefs with a "fanaticism."

Kamehameha V toured the islands to poll his people, who displayed an intense devotion to monarchy and resistance to foreign democracy. When the constitutional convention he convened produced *haole* resentment, but not a constitution, he solely created the Constitution of 1864. Angry *haole* proposed a "military display of power." Kamehameha countered that American and British ships remain at bay. His 1864 Constitution then successfully governed Hawaii for twenty-three years, though political untruths infiltrated the United States. In 1872, with Hawaii against annexation and without a named successor, Kamehameha V died.

Hawaiians voted lineage to elect Lunalilo, who claimed to be heir, but unaccustomed to democratic voting, failed to consider his platform, which pledged return to the Constitution of 1852. He appointed all but one Americans to his cabinet. After only a year and twenty-five days as king, Lunalilo became very ill and died. Cabinet members elected David Kalakaua, who mollified foreign landowners and backed the reciprocity treaty with the United States. Most Hawaiians, including Liliuokalani, did not. They did not understand politics where businessmen were leaders.

In 1876, the US Congress passed a motion honoring the reciprocity treaty that opened the door to annexation. After the king heard of assassination plots, he attempted reforms to re-empower Hawaiians, but he died aboard a ship returning from a US royal visit in 1891. Under the Bayonet Constitution of 1887 that had been forced upon the islanders, Queen Liliuokalani inherited the throne.

The matriarchal society of the islands had all but vanished. For almost fifty years, no woman held a position of political importance. Women were seen as unsuitable for political office. American antipathy toward monarchy, ardor for democracy, and belief in patriarchy led to the statement, "she may reign, but not rule," a posture of political and gender disrespect. Charles Bishop advised her to leave politics and business to the ministers and suggested she would, "live longer and happier ... by not trying to do too much." But do she did.

As princess, she opened a college for Hawaiian girls and a bank for women. As queen, she was a champion to women and for women's rights. She appointed a new cabinet, reappointed her council except for two, requested portfolios from all ministers, and began to enact a more equitable constitution for her people. One of her first official acts designated ten-acre sections of crown land for Hawaiian homesteads: five-years rent-free and one dollar annual per acre thereafter.

It was obvious that her empire was for her people. She polled the population, as had Kamehameha V. Her people wanted "a strong monarchy, a voice for themselves in government, and *no* annexation to a foreign power." Liliuokalani was intelligent, educated, wise, and ethical. Still, after two short years, she was deposed.

President Grover Cleveland believed the overthrow was illegal and offered to give back her throne if she granted amnesty to everyone responsible. She refused his terms. A provisional government was installed with Sanford B. Dole as head of her people. American businessmen who opposed rising tariffs primarily Sanford B. Dole, suggested annexation to protect their investments. Within a year, the Republic of Hawaii was claimed by the US Congress and immediately recognized by the United States government. Hawaii was annexed to the United States in 1898 through a joint resolution of the US Congress.

The queen lived as a private citizen until her death in 1917. In 1993, President Clinton signed the Apology Resolution for the alleged role of the United States in the overthrow of Hawaii's last monarch, Queen Liliuokalani.

Sources: *Scholastic Encyclopedia of Women in the United States* by Sheila Keenan; *The Betrayal of Liliuokalani* by Helena G. Allen; *Hawaii's Story* by Hawaii's Queen Liliuokalani.
November 2006

Chapter Twenty-four:
AstroNOmical WOMEN

~

*H*ypatia of Alexandria was a leading scholar in mathematics and astronomy sixteen hundred years ago. She was author of *The Astronomical Canon* and was a popular university lecturer in philosophy, astronomy, and mathematics. She is credited with geometry and astrometry contributions that were instrumental in the development of the sky-measuring astrolabe. She interpreted Plato and Aristotle to those in Alexandria who inquired. The city loved her, the male rulers envied her, and Bishop Cyril vehemently assailed her. When the university refused his fiat to fire her, he ordered his male monks, to drag her from her chariot into a church where they brutally slashed her to death in the name of God. Bishop Cyril was later elevated to sainthood by the male clergy of the Vatican.

Henrietta Leavitt charted the astronomical skies we see each night. She discovered more than twenty-four hundred variable stars, about half of those then known in 1912. Her most important contribution, her discovery that enabled star distances to be calculated up to ten million light years away, dramatically changed astronomy forever. Her "yardstick to the universe" enabled Edwin Hubble and others to make discoveries that changed our view of the galaxy. Leavitt also developed a standard of photographic magnitude measurements in 1913 that is accepted as "the" standard and is christened the Harvard Standard. But because of her gender, Leavitt was not allowed to pursue her own research studies at the Harvard Observatory. This female astronomer could only research what was assigned to her by the male astronomers. Scientifically restricting her feigned a black hole in the research of our universe. Gender restricting her created unleashed space in which others, otherwise gendered were to soar and explore, famously.

Winifred Edgerton, the first American woman to receive a PhD, earned it cum laude in the masculine field of mathematics and astronomy. Edgerton's application to Columbia College, which had the only telescope at the time, was originally denied because of her gender. But the male professor of astronomy needed an assistant. And, as Edgerton was applying not to the college but to graduate school, the trustees, believing no gender-related precedent would be set, voted to allow her to pursue her advanced studies on a limited tutorial basis. Her work included computations of the orbit of the comet of 1883, and she served on a committee to found Barnard College. Her marriage in 1887 ended her work from which she withdrew due to her husband's objections of the impropriety of committee meetings held in men's offices. When invited by the lieutenant governor to serve on the school board in Albany, her husband deemed it unladylike and forbade her acceptance. She obeyed him. She bore him four children. And she founded the Oaksmere School for girls where she taught for twenty years. In 1926, ten years after his death, she took a position as the librarian at the Barbizon Hotel for women in New York, one of many libraries that might have contained her research, had she been allowed to research.

Maude Bennot remains the only *acting* director in the avant-garde history of Chicago's Adler Planetarium. Established in 1930, the Adler was the first planetarium in the Western Hemisphere. Max Adler had selected the Adler's first director, Philip Fox. When Fox resigned, Maude Bennot, his assistant since the Adler opened, was appointed acting director but never granted full director entitlement, as was Fox and all male directors after her. Upon becoming acting director, a position in which she served for eight years, Bennot, who held a master's in astronomy from Northwestern University, said, "There is a field for women in engineering, astronomy, and other scientific endeavors. But it is definitely limited—mainly … in the minds of men." (*Time* 5/17/37) Bennot's field at the Adler Planetarium in Chicago still stands as a field of directors of men only, with Bennot as the only *acting* director.

Thirteen women between 1960 and 1961, called the *Mercury 13,* secretly and independently of one another trained to be astronauts, but they never became such because they were women. Though experienced pilots—most with more completed flight hours than the *Mercury 7* male astronauts—President Eisenhower clearly stated he wanted only jet test pilots considered for the space program. Jet test pilots were all men. His requirement covertly eliminated all women. In a letter to NASA outlining women's training and drafted for his signature, Vice President Johnson, overt in his tenet on women in the space program, affixed not his signature, but the words, Let's Stop This Now! *Now* lasted twenty-two years until Sally Ride became the first female United States astronaut in space.

Sources: *The Mercury 13*, Martha Ackmann; http://antwrp.gsfc.nasa.gov/apod/ap020113.html;
http://www.adlerplanetarium.org/research/collections/women_in_hist/index.shtml;
http://www.columbia.edu/~rr91/3567/sample_biographies/winifred_edgerton__bio.htm;
http://www.physics.ucla.edu/~cwp/Phase2/Leavitt,_Henrietta_Swan@871234567.html.
December 2006

Eliza Scidmore-Cherry Blossom Trees Advocate
Courtesy DC Public Library, Washingtoniana Division

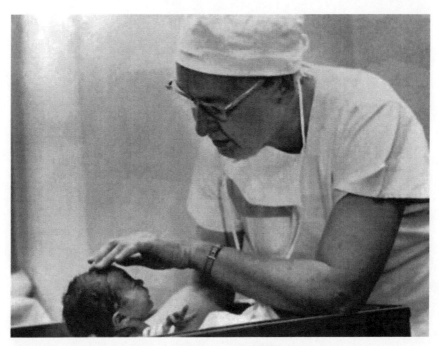

Dr.Virginia Apgar, APGAR Score
Photo by Elizabeth Wilcox. Archives & Special Collections
Columbia University Health Science Library

Emma Lazarus-Lady Liberty Poet
Public Domain

The Salem Martyr by Thomas S. Noble, 1869
Collection of the New York Historical Society

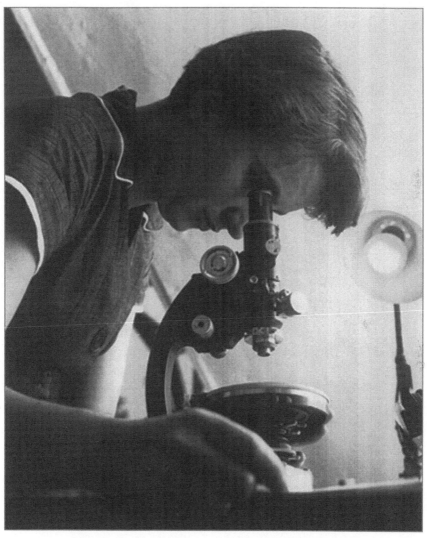

Rosalind Franklin-Molecular Biologist/DNA Researcher
© Henry Grant Collection/Museum of London

Mileva Einstein-Mathematician/Physicist
Swiss National Library–1896
Public Domain

Mary Engle Pennington-Bacteriological Food Chemist
University of Pennsylvania Archives

Queen Liliuokalani-Hawaii
Getty Images

Henrietta Swan Leavitt-Astronomer
© AIP Emilio Segrè Visual Archives, Physics Today Collection
Public Domain

Jo Ann Robinson-Montgomery Bus Boycott
African American Registry

Emily Roebling-Civil Engineer/Brooklyn Bridge
Public Domain

Lady Godiva-Peasant Advocate
by John Collier, Wikimedia Commons
Public Domain

Jane Addams-Social Reformer
Jane Addams Hull-House Museum, UIC Special Collections,
JAMC_0000_0030_1723

Dr. Alice Hamilton-OSHA
LOG-ggbain—DIG 29701

Frances Perkins-Social Security
LOC Prints & Photographs Division, NYWT&S Collection,
[LC-USZ62-111157]

WASP Class of '44-W-3-Julie Stege (front row, third from left)
The Woman's Collection, Texas Woman's University, Denton, Texas

Julia Morgan-Architect
Hearst Castle/California State Parks

Mercury 13-First Lady Astronaut Trainees
NASA

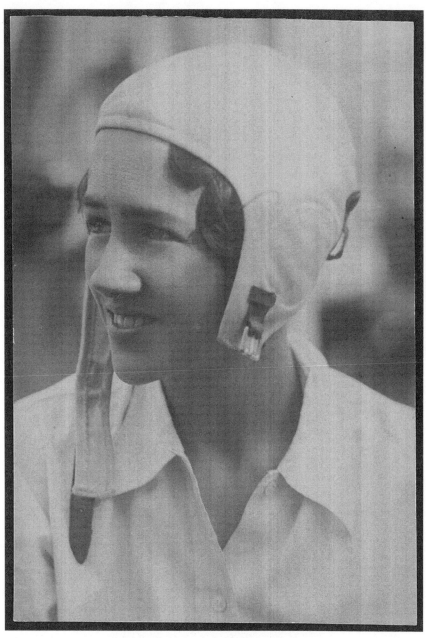

Anne Morrow Lindbergh-Pilot/Author
charleslindbergh.com.images2/china2/L15.jpg

US Representative Patsy Mink-Title IX
Courtesy of Gwendolyn Mink

Hedy Lamarr-Inventor/Cell Phone Technology
Wikimedia Commons
Public Domain

Chapter Twenty-five:
Madame President

~

"*N*one of us could have imagined a woman president," said Rafael Bustillos, a forty-two-year old *huaso* (Chilean cowboy). In 2006, Dr. Michelle Bachelet was elected Chile's first female president.

As minister of health in 2000, Dr. Bachelet, a surgeon, pediatrician, and public health administrator, eliminated the long waiting lines of the sick at government clinics. In 2003, when she was Chile's first female minister of defense and army commander in chief, General Juan Emilio Cheyre pledged to her that the military would "never again" coup nor interfere in politics.

Bachelet's presidential campaign promised dignified pension reform by 2010 to retirees receiving a fraction of what they had been told when the privatization of pension funds that replaced a state social security system failed, a program George W. Bush praised.

Upon taking office, Bachelet immediately appointed ten women and ten men to her cabinet. Many Chileans speak of how good they feel seeing women at top government levels. Many others feel unsettled. In a culture where bias against women runs rampant, where divorce just became legal in 2004, this divorced working mother works as a Chilean president none had imagined.

Sühbaataryn Yanjmaa of Mongolia was the first woman in the world to serve as an acting president during the transitional period of September 1953 to July 1954 in Mongolia.

In the People's Republic of China, with no head of state designate, Song Qingling, widow of Sun Yat-sen founder of the Chinese Republic, and sister-in-law of Chiang Kai-shek, served with Zhu De as vice president and shared presidential duties (1968–1972). In 1980, the People's Republic of China elected her as honorary president.

Isabel Martínez de Perón was the first woman to serve as president of any country. Though not an elected president, as the vice president, she replaced her husband President Juan Perón, upon his death in July 1974. She served until March 1976 as president of Argentina, a country where women first were allowed to vote in 1951.

The first woman to win a democratic presidential election of any country was Vigdis Finnbogadottir, elected president of Iceland in 1980. Three subsequent election victories continued her presidency until 1996.

Globally, approximately forty-six women have served as president or head of state in countries large and small. Bachelet joins ten other female heads of state currently holding office: Ellen Johnson Sirleaf—Liberia; Angela Merkel—Germany; Maria do Carmo Silveira—São Tomé and Principe; Lusia Diogo—Mozambique; Gloria Macapagal-Arroyo—Philippines; Tarja Kaarina Halonen—Finland; Helen Clark—New Zealand; Vaira Vike-Freiberga—Latvia; Mary McAleese—Ireland, and Khaleda Zia—Bangladesh.

In 2007, Ségoléne Royal ran as France's first female presidential candidate from a major political party. In 2006, the French cabinet approved a proposal to encourage political parties to promote more women. If it passes, districts with more than thirty-five hundred people will be obliged to ensure gender parity of appointments to top positions beginning in 2008. Fifty-six political parties in twenty-four other countries already employ a gender quota system. Some are Belgium, Brazil, South Africa, Nepal, Denmark, Norway, India, and Sweden,

In 2004, newly elected prime minister of Spain, Jose Luis Rodriguez Zapatero, fulfilled his campaign promise and appointed eight female ministers to achieve a gender equitable cabinet. Marta Oritz, a women's rights activist since Franco died in 1975, could not imagine this political parity would happen.

Of the first 12,000 members to serve in the US Congress, only 215 were women—11,785 were men; of 110 Supreme Court justices, only two were women. In the 110th Congress, only 16 US senators will be women, and of 435 representatives in the House, only 71 will be women. Nine women will serve as governor, none as president.

The Chilean cowboy's reaction of a woman president, none could have imagined is still to be imagined in the North American country of cowboys and women.

Source: http://www.terra.es/personal2/monolith/00women2.htm.
January 2007

Note: Women's History does NOT repeat itself: Cristina Fernandez de Kirchner, Argentina's first elected female president in December 2007, became the first female president of any country to be reelected in October 2011.

Chapter Twenty-six:
Civil Rights Women
~

S eventy-three years predating Rosa Parks, a refined teacher sat in the first-class ladies' car on a train in Tennessee. When told to move to the smoker car for Negroes, Ida B. Wells politely refused. She had a first-class ticket, she was a lady, and she planned to stay in her ticketed seat. Dragged to the dirty smoker car as white passengers cheered, she got off at the next stop. Wells was well within her rights. The Civil Rights Act of 1875 banned discrimination on public transportation. Wells filed a lawsuit and won. She later sued in a repeat situation and won, which inspired others. Her disclosures on the lynching of black men initiated the nation's antilynching campaign in 1882.

The NAACP began as an interracial organization in a 1909 meeting initiated by Mary White Ovington, a white woman in New York, between a representative of the New York City mayor's office and author/abolitionist William Walling. Ovington saw to it that over a third in positions were women, one was Ida B. Wells. The NAACP ceased being mostly interracial in the 1930s, excluding Ovington from some of her civil rights work.

Pauli Murray attempted to break the color line in education at the University of North Carolina Law School in 1938, but was denied admission. As a Howard University Law School student in Washington, DC, Murray organized a cafeteria sit-in. After four hours of orderly protest, the demonstrators were served. Civil rights were gained. But in 1944, people did not talk about this. The press ignored the story. Those courageous young blacks sitting-in at lunch counters in the 1960s were ahead of their time. Murray was two decades ahead of them.

In 1949, Jo Ann Robinson, who recently moved to Montgomery to accept a teaching position at Alabama State University, sat on a nearly empty bus. Ignoring the driver's order to move, she fled in terror as he came at her. The horror of that experience never left her, and it caused her to advocate for bus desegregation. Robinson wrote of a bus boycott to Montgomery's mayor in 1954 if abuse toward black passengers continued. The night of Rosa Parks' arrest in 1955, Robinson printed 52,500 flyers calling for a boycott urging blacks to stay off the buses. Whites joined with blacks and shut down the public transit system. Thirteen months later, the US Supreme Court declared racial segregation on public transportation throughout the South unconstitutional. Parks and Robinson's initial actions ignited the organized civil rights movement.

Daisy Bates and her husband started a black newspaper in the 1940s addressing issues as slums, police brutality, legal injustices, hiring discrimination, and school desegregation. In 1957, as president of the Arkansas NAACP, Bates accompanied nine teenagers to the entrance of Central High School to desegregate Little Rock's school system. They were blocked from entering by the National Guard called out by Governor Orval Faubus. Faubus was cited for contempt, and federal troops were ordered to escort the students into school. A white woman representing Southern Christian women warned Bates to withdraw from the students or be destroyed. Bates stayed. Her paper's advertisers were threatened with attack. They canceled their advertisements and forced Bates to shut down her paper but not her activism.

Fannie Lou Hamer began her civil rights work in 1962 when, at age forty-five, she attended her first political rally and learned she had the right to vote. This transformed her into a leader. She joined with other blacks to try to register to vote. Afterward, her boss angry that she had tried to register fired her from her job of eighteen years. Her husband and daughter also lost their jobs and were arrested, she was shot at, and police officers entered her house without a warrant, but that did not stop her activism. Because blacks were barred from the Democratic Party, she helped form the Mississippi Freedom Democratic Party. They established a Washington office and several states endorsed them.

Hamer co-chaired a MFDP delegation to the 1964 Democratic National Convention and spoke before the credentials committee on national TV challenging the all-white Mississippi delegation. They had covert support from Lyndon Johnson, but to preserve his presidential nomination, he overtly worked against their convention participation. She met with Hubert Humphrey, who indicated how he supported them in his heart, but could not jeopardize a chance to be on the ticket with Johnson. She questioned his position to be on the ballot verses the lives of four hundred thousand black citizens. Unsuccessful at being seated, she was successful when the party pledged not to seat any delegations at the 1968 convention that excluded black Americans.

In the 1963 March on Washington, not one activist woman marched down Constitution Avenue with the men. Not one woman spoke. Not one woman went to the White House with the men to meet President John F. Kennedy. Black civil rights activist women faced double discrimination fighting for racial rights with whites and for gender justice with men in the civil rights movement. Martin Luther King, Jr., delivered ardent speeches as he spoke the voice given to the civil rights movement by Ida B. Wells, Mary Ovington, Pauli Murray, Rosa Parks, Jo Ann Robinson, Daisy Bates, Fannie Lou Hamer, and countless unheralded women of the civil rights movement.

Sources: *The Montgomery Bus Boycott and the Women Who Started It*, Jo Ann Gibson Robinson; *Pauli Murray: The Autobiography of a Black Activist, Feminist, Lawyer, Priest, and Poet*, Pauli Murray; *Freedom's Daughters: The Unsung Heroines of the Civil Rights Movement from 1830 to 1970*, Lynne Olson; *Women in the Civil Rights Movement: Trailblazers & Torchbearers 1941–1965*. Eds. Vicki L. Crawford, Jacqueline Anne Rouse, and Barbara Woods. February 2007

Chapter Twenty-seven:
Bags to Bridges

 ∾

From Brooklyn to Manhattan, a bridge spanning the East River seemed daring and impossible in 1865. But Emily Roebling's father-in-law John drew the plans and lobbied four years to receive government approval, only to die a month later. It befell Washington, his son, to superintend construction, but challenges regarding his abilities arose. Emily, the first woman to do so, addressed the American Society of Civil Engineers to keep the project in the Roebling family. She was skilled in mathematics, material strengths, catenary curves, and cable construction. It was rumored that Emily was the brains behind the civil engineering of the Brooklyn Bridge.

She became the "man on the job" just three years into the eleven-year construction project when a decompression disease left Washington partially paralyzed, deaf, unable to speak, and confined to bed. Every day she inspected the work and dispatched construction questions from bridge officials, representatives, and contractors. Many thought she was the chief engineer, but she did not have the title. Washington monitored progress from his window afar, as Emily oversaw the actual construction project. The most adroit architectural drawings do not morph into monumental structures without equally adroit civil engineering.

When the bridge opened in 1883, the Honorable Abram S. Hewitt cited Emily and Washington both equally for its construction. Plaques in both bridge towers honor her skills. Still, Emily's name is sparsely, if at all, included in most references to the Brooklyn Bridge, a bridge John Roebling put on paper and Emily Roebling put over water.

Margaret Knight, recognized as the "female Edison" holds eighty-seven US patents. Her interest in machines and her natural ability to create was evidenced early. Born into a poor New England family in 1838, she worked in the cotton mills when she was nine years old. At age twelve, after watching a spindle twirl off its moorings and horrifyingly injure a little girl, Knight invented a safety device. The device automatically shut down machines to prevent injuries, and was installed on all looms in Manchester, New Hampshire. It is in standard use today.

Her inventions include the window frame and sash, a spinning and a sewing machine, a machine for cutting shoe soles and five other pieces of equipment for shoe manufacturing, and a boring tool. She designed a compound rotary engine whose rights she handed to the Knight-Davidson Motor Company in New York. But her greatest invention that affected all our lives is the machine that folds and glues paper into the square bottom paper bag. Until her invention of 1868, paper bags were envelope v-shaped and made by machine. Flat-bottom bags, made by hand, were very costly, and thus very rare.

During her first week of work in a paper bag company, Knight thought it unusual there was not a machine to fold and glue the flat-bottom bags that functioned better than v-shaped bags. Knight made machine drawings, performed experiments, and built a wooden model that produced thousands of flat-bottom bags. She hired a machinist to cast the iron model needed to apply for a patent. Charles Annan saw her machine being cast into iron, copied it, and received its patent.

Knight, the first woman to appear before the commissioner of patents in Washington, DC, fought for her invention evidencing her drawings, records, photos, models, folded bags, and witnesses. The ruling came in her favor.

Founder of the Eastern Paper Bag Company in 1870, workmen installing her equipment reportedly refused her advice griping, "What does a woman know about machines?" Even the Smithsonian did not include her models for preservation in the early 1900s. Not until 1979, when the Smithsonian was seeking original inventions of women, was her patent model found and included.

Knight is one of twelve women honorably inducted into The National Inventors Hall of Fame that honorably inducted 316 men.

Sources: *Girls Think of Everything,* Catherine Thimmesh; *The Great Bridge: The Epic Story of the Building of the Brooklyn Bridge,* David McCullough; http://www.bookpage.com/0603bp/children/marvelous_mattie.html. March 2007

Chapter Twenty-eight:
Taxes a La Godiva

~

*L*egend portrays Lady Godiva as a proficient horsewoman who enjoyed the hunt. But popular legend lacks in the complete portrayal of this fine person.

She was a woman of personal wealth and good fortune with a strong interest in the arts and society. She was widowed in the eleventh century Coventry, England. Her second husband, Leofric, Earl of Mercia, had been given a public affairs position in government with responsibilities for matters of finance. In this role, he developed a manic involvement in public works programs that he funded by placing taxes on every commodity possible.

Together as a couple, they generously endowed several monasteries to serve the spiritual needs of the town. Individually, Lady Godiva attempted to foster an interest in art among the peasants to serve their cultural needs. She achieved little success, however, because the peasants did not have time to pursue cultural interests. They needed to work endlessly just to survive due to the heavy taxes Leofric had placed on necessities such as food, clothes, and shelter.

Lady Godiva sympathized with the peasants and wanted to enrich their lives. She did not approve of the total repression of cultural art programs by the numerous taxed municipal water works projects. She chastised men for their functional priorities that completely ignored the social and artistic needs of the citizens. According to her philosophy, public responsibilities and appreciation of the arts did not cancel out one another, but were necessary and compatible in a tandem partnership for true civic development and enrichment. Taxes would have to be lowered.

She presented a tax reduction proposal to Leofric at his village hall bureau. It is written that he broke out in loud and insulting laughter from

109

which he fell off his stool, injured his wrist, and had to be assisted upright. Not only would he not sanction a tax reduction, he added a new tax, a tax on paintings. Since only Lady Godiva and the church owned paintings, with the church tax exempt, his new tax befell only on her.

Their different perspectives grew into a marital war of wills. Although Leofric continued to resist her pleadings, she did not relent. Eventually, he conceded but with a clause. He would reduce some of the tax burdens on the peasants for whom she advocated, but not without a compromise on her part.

Leofric asserted how the highest form of art proclaimed by the ancient Greeks was that of the nude body. If his wife truly believed in her cultural cause for the poor, she would present herself to the town as an example of this highest form of art and ride naked upon a horse in full light of day to prove her intentions honorable. His proviso simulated a common practice for penitents who would publicly process through town in shame, nearly naked, in a sleeveless white garment.

Aware that her long tresses could cover her discreetly, Lady Godiva held Leofric to his word. She issued a proclamation that all people were to remain indoors with windows shuttered during her ride. Thus, she rode with dignity, in the manner of a penitent, that a reduction in taxes could be achieved. Touched by her benevolent act, Leofric agreed not just to lessen taxes but also to remove all that he had imposed during his tenure. According to legend, a tailor named Tom bore a hole in his shutters to peep as she rode, and he was struck blind.

Lady Godiva is celebrated in countless words and works of art for her beauty, her nakedness, her indecency, her daring in the year 1067. But legend is scant of acknowledgment given to her purpose of lessening the oppressive tax burdens placed on the poor, or to the proviso of her ride placed on her—both put in place by her husband.

Sources: http://abacom.com/~jkrause/godiva.html; http://en.wikipedia.org/wiki/Lady_Godiva.
April 2007

Chapter Twenty-nine:
Jane & Gender

In her own words, she was an utter failure. Albeit, she had thrived in college, was class president, valedictorian of her class, as well as student magazine editor, but as an 1881 college graduate, a woman of high intelligence with a strong inner drive to do meaningful work, she was stifled.

Jane Addams was of the first generation of college-educated women to graduate into a patriarchal world where no positions awaited them. They were considered a malady. College educated men, graduates from Harvard founded in 1636 and all other men only universities were, and long had been, the norm.

College admissions first opened to women in 1833. at Oberlin College in Ohio. By 1867, only twenty-two colleges had followed suit. These new educated women with aspirations other than marriage were abusively labeled as selfish, abusively treated vindictively, and abusively shunned for their aptitudes. They were told not only that they could not but that they should not.

Harvard physician Edward Clark warned that intellectual activity particularly that of higher education would have a detrimental effect on women's health and well-being. Mysterious mental and physical distress disorders began to appear and became pandemic in young educated women. Symptoms could not be traced anatomically. (*) They were labeled neurasthenia by neurologist George Beard, who cited one of the causes to be an increase in mental activity among women. In response to such unfounded gender tocsins, seventeen college-educated women further defied convention and formed the American Association of University Women (**) to encourage college education and to develop employment opportunities for women.

In this climate of ubiquitous female gender defame, Addams, herself, suffered severe physical illness and mental depression. She was confined to a clinic for six weeks of treatment under the care of the leading expert on neurasthenia, Doctor Silas Weir Mitchell. His cure was total seclusion, confined bed rest with no reading or writing, and elimination of all use of body and brain. Post treatment, Dr. Mitchell prescribed no more than two hours of intellectual stimulation per day and cautioned women never to use pen, brush, or pencil. (***)

For eight years of Addams' young adult life, this ambitious, intelligent woman (as many women of the era) questioned her sanity, her passion to perform, and the restrictive realities of Victorian female's submissiveness to Victorian males and mores. Her post college years were painfully whiled away, her intellectual abilities in check.

On one of her travels abroad, she visited Toynbee Hall in London, a settlement house run by educated young men aiding the poor in an interactive manner that appeared to benefit the educated young men even more than it benefited the poor. She saw in Toynbee a vision for her future. She would reconstruct this model in Chicago but with one difference. Her settlement would provide outreach opportunities for college women as well as outreach opportunities for the poor.

The programs initiated by Hull House women in 1889 are now considered basic: kindergartens, playgrounds, nurseries, and a gymnasium and after school programs. That is, art classes, drama classes, ESL, college extension courses, citizenship classes, the first Boy Scout troop, etc. They provided opportunities rather than aid and encouraged cross-class interactions. These privileged women believed people from differing classes learned from one another. They interacted with the poorest of the poor, particularly the unassimilated immigrants who struggled with second language challenges on top of impoverished living conditions.

In her own words, Addams opened Hull House to save herself as much as to save the poor. In so doing, she also saved the mental health of all the women who found meaningful work with other like-minded women at Hull House and exponentially, she saved the mental health of a wealth of women on into the twenty-first century who walk through doors she opened. By the turn of the century, Addams was an AAUW Chicago member.

Venerated for Hull House, Nobel-Prized for Peace, Jane Addams never has been recognized for the gender steps she took, and the gender paths she paved. That has changed thanks to five students and one teacher in rural America who discovered that no legal holiday in the entire United States honors a woman and then worked with local AAUW Illinois members to institute such a day.

Henceforth, December 10 in Illinois, decreed by legislation, honors Jane Addams, a woman who surmounted (previously) insurmountable gender confines placed on her because she was a woman, a woman who was an utter success.

(*) Similar to symptoms identified in homemakers as the "problem that has no name," by Betty Friedan in the *Feminine Mystique,* 1963.
(**) AAUW, a national association with a membership of approximately 100,000.
(***) Charlotte Perkins Gilman, "The Yellow Wallpaper," captures the horror of this cure.

Sources: *A Useful Woman: The Early Life of Jane Addams,* Gioia Diliberto; Women Building Chicago 1790–1990 Eds: Rima Lunin Schultz & Adele Hast; *Degrees of Equality,* Susan Levine.
June 2007

Chapter Thirty:
Oh She/OSHA

❧

*R*ecognized as the founder of occupational medicine, Dr. Alice Hamilton was the first American physician—male or female—to specialize in the medical practice of occupational health. She developed this specialization during the years she lived at Hull House.

After graduating from the University of Michigan Medical School in 1893, Dr. Hamilton served internships in Minneapolis and Boston, and then a year of medical studies at universities in Munich and Leipzig where previously men had kept out women. As the first female the men allowed in, Dr. Hamilton received permission to attend lectures only in bacteriology and pathology, and only if she would remain invisible to male students and professors.

Once back in America, Dr. Hamilton accepted a pathology professorship at the Women's Medical College of Northwestern University in Evanston, Illinois, and moved into Hull House where she stayed for more than twenty years. She lived with other intelligent women and interacted with the poor. This experience shaped her and her work.

She observed how immigrant workers severely infected or maimed at work, were routinely fired and forgotten, and new immigrants were hired. As the industrial era developed, government, employers, and workers were unprepared for this new way of life. Regulatory health and safety conditions were not yet identified or legislated, that is, until Dr. Alice Hamilton entered the scene.

During the 1902 typhoid fever epidemic in Chicago, she accepted a position as a bacteriologist at Chicago's Memorial Institute for Infectious Diseases. There she discovered the corollary between sewage and flies in the transmission of typhoid. She scientifically linked many health disabilities to noxious chemical exposure and unsafe working conditions in factories.

As the first director of the Illinois Occupational Disease Commission established in 1910, she conducted a statewide survey in which she inspected more than three hundred industrial sites, and discovered more than seventy industrial conditions that exposed workers to lead poisoning. Her report brought about the first Illinois law providing workplace health compensation. Extensive legislative regulatory measures followed.

After presenting her report at an international conference in Brussels, she received an offer to expand her research to a national level from Charles O'Neill, commissioner of labor in the US Department of Commerce. But he did not offer her a salary or a position. With few opportunities offered, or even available to women, she accepted, and from 1911 until 1921 she implemented innovative procedural changes in factories across the nation. In retrospect, she is considered the first OSHA volunteer inspector.

In 1919, Harvard Medical School offered Dr. Hamilton an assistant professorship of industrial medicine, with provisions concerning her gender, though not her abilities. She was not to use the faculty club, was not offered tickets to football games, and was not to march with male professors at commencement ceremonies. She accepted this work under these gender-abusive, anti-female working conditions, well aware that all her students would be of the male gender. Harvard Medical School did not admit students who were female until 1945 (and not at all Harvard colleges until 1975).

While at Harvard, she was able to continue her national industrial research and after six years, joined the faculty of Harvard's School of Public Health. From 1924 to 1930, she served on the League of Nations Health Committee and expanded her research internationally. In 1935, she retired from Harvard, worked as a consultant for the US Labor Department in its division of labor standards, and served as president of the National Consumers League from 1944 to 1949.

Dr. Hamilton said many viewed her concern for worker health and safety in industrial medicine as tainted with socialism or with feminine sentimentality for the poor. But her radical ideas for workplace reform became the philosophy that governs occupational health and safety standards today. In 1970, the Occupational Safety and Health Act was signed into law by then-president Richard M. Nixon, three months after her death at age 101.

Dr. Hamilton received many awards, distinctions, and numerous honorary degrees for her work that saved thousands, if not millions, of lives. However, her rank at Harvard remains, *Assistant* Professor Emeritus of Industrial Medicine. Oh she, OSHA notwithstanding, was never granted a full professorship equal to her male colleagues, none of whom had ever been exposed to the occupational health hazard of gender restrictions as was (and still is) she, the first American physician to specialize in occupational health.

Sources: www.cdc.gov/niosh/hamilton/hamhist.html; www.osha.gov /Publications/JSHQ/spring2002/hamilton.htm.
July 2007

Chapter Thirty-one:
Her Social Securi-Tea

~

*T*he unthankful issue was her gender. There were repeated demands for her resignation. Still, in 1929, as the first female US cabinet member, thus, the first woman to be in the presidential line of succession, Secretary of Labor Frances Perkins coauthored much New Deal legislation. She was the chief architect of the Social Security Act and chairwoman of the President's Committee that wrote this legislation.

Excerpts from her words follow: The beginnings of old-age insurance came about largely, I think, by the crisis of the times. Where did the idea come from? I don't know. I must have picked it up in the general reading that one does; in the general conversation with other socially minded, intelligent, and educated people. (She had worked and lived with the college-educated women at Hull House in Chicago.)

Before I was appointed, I had a little conversation with [FDR] Roosevelt in which I said perhaps he didn't want me to be Secretary of Labor because if I were, I should want to do this, and this, and this. Among the things I wanted to do was find a way of getting unemployment, old age, and health insurance. He said, "Well, do you think *it* can be done?"

I said, "I don't know."

He said, "Well, there are constitutional problems, aren't there?"

"Yes, very severe constitutional problems," I said. "But what have we been elected for except to solve the constitutional problems?"

"Well," he said, "do you think *you* can do it?"

"I don't know," I said. But I wanted to try. "I want to know if I have your authorization."

He looked at me and nodded wisely. "All right," he said. "I will authorize you to try and if you succeed, that's fine."

This was the way it all began, just a little committee to explore the subject. He didn't like the word "social" so we had a Committee on Economic Security. The greatest problem was the constitutional one. How could you get around this business of the state-federal relationships? It seemed that could not be done. It had been really a tough fight in committee.

One day I went out to tea … in Washington, you don't go to parties because you want to. I had to call on the wife of the Supreme Court Justice. I went to her house and presented myself. There were a lot of other people there, and I met Mr. Justice Stone, who had just come home from the court and was getting his cup of tea. We greeted each other and sat down and had a little chat.

He said, "How are you getting on?"

I said, "All right." Then I said, "Well, you know, we are having big troubles, Mr. Justice, because in this draft of the Economic Security Act, which we are working on, we are not quite sure what will be a wise method of establishing this law. It is a very difficult constitutional problem." He looked around as if to see if anyone was listening, then confidentially, he said, "The taxing power, my dear, the taxing power. You can do anything under the taxing power." I did not question him further.

I went back to my committee and said I was firmly for the taxing power of the United States. You can do anything under it, I said. The whole system of taxation is the basis of the Social Security Act. We voted once to have a federal system, and then in a couple of hours, thought we ought to meet again, so we would meet and we would vote the other way, a federal-state system. Then we would review it again, and we would meet again. This went on for weeks. When the report had to go in within a week, I asked them to come to my house, not for dinner but after dinner, and then I told them I was going to lock the door, and we would stay until we had settled it and there would be no more review. This was the final and the last meeting.

We then did a great deal of educating, chiefly through hearings, public hearings in the Senate. I made over one hundred speeches, practically every member made many speeches. The result was a bill that finally was presented to Congress, debated very briefly, and we gave way on all kinds of things. We gave way on universal health insurance, just so we could get the basis of the bill. And we did get the bill passed in August 1935 by an extraordinary vote. (The vote was 371 to 33 in the House, and 77 to 6 in the Senate.)

Then began the great problem—the administration of this act. Thousands of problems arose, the act had to be amended, and has been amended, and amended, and amended, until it has now grown into a large and important project, for which, I think the people of the United States are deeply thankful. [Rescinding, this author suspects, the unthankful issue of her gender.]

At the time of her death, Secretary of Labor Willard Wirtz said, "Every man and woman who works for a living wage, under safe conditions, for reasonable hours, or is protected by unemployment compensation of Social Security, is her debtor."

Sources: Complete text at: http://www.ssa.gov/history/perkins5.html; "The Roots of Social Security" by Frances Perkins; Delivered at Social Security Administration Headquarters-- Baltimore, Maryland 10/23/1962 http://www.dol.gov/oasam/programs/history/perkins.htm. August 2007

Chapter Thirty-two:
Mostly Men, Women, and Children
~

*H*ull House in Chicago was a female endeavor established to address inhumane living conditions created by rapid, uncontrolled industrialization. The women of Hull House developed civic, social, and workplace prototypes that became the foundation for government today. They were of the first generation of women politically active at city, state, and federal levels.

In 1891, Florence Kelley fled an abusive husband and moved into Hull House with her three children. Soon after, she began working for the Illinois Bureau of Labor Statistics, and in 1893, was appointed Illinois' first Chief Factory Inspector by Governor John Altgeld. Her investigations on slums and the garment industry centered on women and children, mostly children, some as young as three who worked in tenement sweatshops. Seminal labor laws followed her investigative disclosures.

Illinois regulated sweatshops, limited women's working hours, and passed the first state law setting a legal age (fourteen) for child employment. Witnessing countless cases against sweatshops fail in the courts impelled Kelley to complete her law degree (1894), and she was admitted to the bar.

In 1899, she created the National Consumers League and moved with her children to New York as its first general-secretary, a position she held her lifetime. Through the NCL, she instituted the use of clothing labels to identify legally produced goods, she promoted companies that met government standards, and she encouraged consumers to boycott sweatshop products. During her administration, workplace regulations that transformed manufacturing conditions in America were established. She was an author of the Pure Food and Drug Act of 1906, forerunner of the FDA, as well as laws that regulated work hours and established minimum wage.

In her efforts to eliminate child labor, she advocated for mandatory school attendance. She organized the New York Child Labor Committee and called for a commission at the federal level to legislate child labor laws. With her colleague Lillian Wald, Kelley formally proposed a federal commission to male legislators, whose laws appeared apathetic to the death rate of working children—680 daily. Congress enacted her proposal and established the US Children's Bureau in 1912. President William Howard Taft appointed Julia Lathrop the bureau's first director, and thus, the first woman to be a US bureau chief.

However, government appointments were not new to this Hull House woman. Governor Altgeld had appointed Lathrop to head the Illinois Board of Charities in 1892 in recognition of her survey, "Hull House Maps and Papers," which documented the squalor inflicting the city's poor. This appointment made her the first Hull House woman, but not the last, to hold a government position.

As head of this Illinois board, Lathrop recommended separate care facilities for the mentally ill, the aged, the sick, and the disabled. All were being housed and treated together. In Chicago, with other Hull House women, she founded the first juvenile court in the United States. It had a psychiatric clinic for the young wrongdoers, mostly poor-immigrant children. Lathrop relentlessly advocated against capital punishment for juveniles and was a trustee of the Immigrants' Protection League.

As director of the US Children's Bureau in Washington, DC, Lathrop pioneered detailed studies on illegitimacy, baby and mother mortality, child labor, juvenile delinquency, and pensions for mothers. One of her first accomplishments was the creation and distribution of free pamphlets on the health needs of pregnant women and the care of babies. During her nine-year tenure, the Keating-Owen Child Labor Act of 1916 was passed. It prohibited interstate commerce of goods manufactured by children, and the Child Labor Division was created to enforce the act.

Lathrop served as president of the National Conference for Social Work in 1918 and 1919. After World War I, President Woodrow Wilson commissioned her and Grace Abbott, another social worker and Hull House woman to an international conference on child welfare in Europe where Lathrop helped create a new childcare bureau in Czechoslovakia, itself newly created.

The Sheppard-Towner Act, which provided states with grant money to develop programs of health care for mothers and children, was legislated in 1921, due mostly to the actions of Lathrop and her colleagues, mostly women. The American Medical Association, mostly men, labeled the law socialistic, and the women who supported it as sinister Communist conspirators.

Upon her appointment in 1925 to the Child Welfare Committee formed by the League of Nations, Lathrop traveled again to Europe to represent the United States at the League of Nations Childcare Commission. She served on the CWC through 1931, the year before her death at age seventy-four.

Sources: http://www.webster.edu/~woolflm/lathrop.html;
http://www.webster.edu/~woolflm/kelley.html#worksc.
September 2007

Chapter Thirty-three:
The Missing Peace
~

S he was called a traitor in 1915 for her pacifist opposition to World War I. Her name was on the Senate Judiciary Committee's traitor list in 1919. Still she was adamant that no matter the cause, the pain of the fight would render meaningless the victory. She was convinced that only peace and democracy would bring peace and democracy. Her name was on another list in 1931, that of Nobel Peace Prize winners, as the first American woman to receive the Nobel Peace Prize. Her name? Jane Addams.

Another pacifist, Countess Bertha Kinsky was born of aristocracy in 1876 in Prague, which then was part of the Austrian Empire. She grew up learning languages, studying the classics, and preparing to be an opera singer. But as a young woman, with family fortunes squandered, she had to earn her living. She first worked as a governess in Austria, and then for a mere eight days as secretary-housekeeper to Alfred Nobel in Paris. It is speculated she departed his employ quickly, perhaps rejecting his attentions and marriage proposal, for it was known she loved another.

Upon her return to Austria, she married Arthur von Suttner and began her career as a journalist and author. In her book, *The Machine Age*, she published radical views on education and women's rights. She became a pacifist and envisioned an international peace league to arbitrate instead of to war. Largely through her efforts, the International Peace Bureau was formed with her as vice-president. She became known as Peace Bertha. In 1899, she led two hundred women to the First Hague Conference, but was the only woman allowed in the conference. Her work there laid the foundation for the League of Nations and the United Nations.

Her anti-militarism book, *Die Waffen neider!* (*Lay Down Your Arms!*) though extremely controversial, was extremely successful and translated into twelve languages. She became a sought-after speaker promoting peace, and she founded the Austrian Peace Society. She and Alfred Nobel corresponded until his death. It is believed she was the impetus in his decision to establish a prize for peace for deserving people, be they "Swede or foreigner, man or woman." Upon his death on December 10, 1896, Nobel left his entire fortune to create the foundation that annually honors men and women for outstanding contributions. In accord with a choice he would have endorsed, Baroness Bertha von Suttner was the first woman awarded the Nobel Peace Prize in 1905.

On December 14, 1914, in a letter to suffragist Carrie Chapman Catt, Jane Addams wrote of her dedication to "the cause of peace." At the end of that year, they wrote to women's groups around the country inviting them to meet early the following year in Washington, DC to consider organizing a National Peace Committee. In April of 1915 at the Hague, Addams convened with more than one thousand women from eleven European countries and the United States at the International Congress of Women to stop the savageness of World War I. They formed a Women's Committee for Permanent Peace (WPP). Addams was its first president.

Their peace efforts did not keep the United States from entering World War I. However, women's valor for the value of peace was winning regard. On April 2, 1917 in Washington, DC, forty-nine US Congressmen and US Congresswoman Jeannette Rankin, the first woman elected to the House, cast fifty votes against US entry into the war. Though not reelected, Rankin continued to advocate for peace. In 1919, she joined Addams in Zurich, Switzerland, as a delegate to the Second International Congress of Women, where Addams reorganized the WPP into the Women's International League for Peace and Freedom. The WILPF was founded to awaken awareness on the causes and concept of war, to abolish war completely, and to work ceaselessly for world peace based on justice and respect for human rights.

The American Legion's male members considered the WILPF members radical and publicly attempted to portray them as dangerous, unpatriotic females. But the legion's accusations were debased as President Calvin Coolidge upheld Addams and her peace efforts.

After 1920, Addams came to be recognized as the greatest woman of the progressive era. In 1931, she was awarded the Nobel Peace Prize, principally for founding the WILPF. Born in 1860, Jane Addams died of cancer in 1935.

In Chicago, artifacts and Hull House itself are preserved in the Hull-House Museum. Addams' social programs of opportunities that respect the dignity of the less fortunate, especially immigrants, continue through the Hull House Association. As well, the WILPF is still active, still seeking the missing peace.

Sources: *The Book of Distinguished American Women*, Vincent Wilson, Jr.; *Champion of Democracy*, Dennis Brindell Fradin & Judith Bloom Fradin; http://en.citizendium.org/wiki/Jane_Addams; http://jofreeman.com/photos/CodePink.html.
October 2007

Chapter Thirty-four:
War and Women's Peace

~

*T*he antiwar Greek comedy *Lysistrata* by Aristophanes (411 BCE) tells of the women who barricaded the public funds forums and withheld sex from the husbands to end the Peloponnesian War and to procure peace. *Lysistrata,* the story's protagonist who leads the women, translates to, "she who disbands armies."

Wu Zetian was the only female in Chinese history to rule China effectively. She was emperor during a peaceful and culturally diverse Tang dynasty, from 618 to 906, and her reign was a time of relative freedom for women. Contrary to Confucian beliefs against rule by women, Wu elevated women's positions. They contributed to culture and politics and did not bind their feet or lead submissive lives. Wu professed the ideal ruler was one who ruled like a mother over her children. She reduced the army's size and stopped the influence of aristocratic military men by replacing them with a government run by scholars. Fair to peasants, Wu lowered oppressive taxes, raised agricultural production, and strengthened public works. Wu Zetian died peacefully at age eighty in 705 CE.

The Lovedu were a society of single mothers in South Africa around 1600. They lived by traditionally feminine ideals of peace, tolerance, compromise, and cooperation under the rule of Modjadji queens. The queen who needed no army was dubbed devious and evil by European invaders who could not break through her diplomatic skill to avoid war. Male Boer traders considered her pacifist stance immoral. But Africans considered her a wise ruler and paid her homage. In the 1890s, armed Boer settlers attacked and claimed much Lovedu lands. Still, Modjadji III, ruled peacefully.

American women formed the Female Peace Society in 1820. The European Women's Peace League, established in 1854 by Swedish feminist

Fredrika Bremer, was the first transnational peace group. Bremer said, "Separately we are weak and can achieve only a little, but if we extend our hands around the whole world, we should be able to take the earth in our hands like a little child." International antiwar movements were on the rise. Women of diverse backgrounds from multiple countries bonded in international womanship for peace.

Lucretia Mott was one of the leaders of the Universal Peace Union (UPU) founded after the Civil War in 1866. It grew out of the American Peace Society adopted during the Civil War. The UPU membership was gender equal as were its leaders. They labored to remove the causes of war and to abash all resorts to deadly force. They promoted principles of love and nonviolence, immediate disarmament, and a general arbitration treaty among nations. Because of them, laws in Pennsylvania regarding conscientious objectors were minimized.

Despite the terrible carnage of the American Civil War that left American women grieving the loss of life and wanting another way to resolve conflicts, Julia Ward Howe wrote "The Battle Hymn of the Republic." However, five years later, reading of the Franco-Prussian War that devastated much of Europe awakened a consciousness in her. Howe questioned herself not only as to why is it that nations do this to one another, but also what might women do to spoil the spoils of war. She wrote her Mother's Day Proclamation to women worldwide of their sacred right as mothers to protect the human life. She traveled to London in 1872 to initiate a Women's Peace Congress and began observing Mother's Day devoted to the advocacy of peace doctrines.

In 1917 Russia, with two million soldiers dead in the war and with living conditions abhorrent, Russian women united in a strike for "bread and peace." Men joined them and on the following day, crowds had swelled. Virtually every industry, shop, and enterprise had ceased to function. Almost the entire populace went on strike. Czar Nicholas I ordered military intervention, however, the military was no longer loyal. More than eighty thousand troops mutinied or joined the demonstrations. Four days later, Nicholas was forced to abdicate and the provisional government granted women the right to vote.

Women for Peace cofounded by Bella Abzug in 1971, is often cited as a factor in the adoption of the Limited Test Ban Treaty. Among the first Americans to oppose the Vietnam War, Abzug called for Nixon's impeachment. She was elected to Congress in 1970 on a strong feminist peace platform. Her first official act demanded a date for US withdrawal from Vietnam.

Sources: *Looking for Lovedu*, Ann Jones; http://www.womeninworldhistory.com/heroine6.html http://womenshistory.about.com/gi/dynamic/offsite.htm?zi=1/XJ/Ya&sdn=womenshistory&cdn=education&tm=37&f=11&tt=14&bt=1&bts=1&zu=http%3A//www.swarthmore.edu/Library/peace/DG026-050/DG038UPU.html; http://en.wikipedia.org/wiki/Women_Strike_for_Peace.
November 2007

Chapter Thirty-five:
Women Airforce Service Pilots

~

*A*nd when they died, they were denied military recognition, honors, and burials because the men in the US military would not accept female pilots, albeit there were not enough male pilots.

Jacqueline Cochran founded WASP, a 1943 program of volunteer female civilian pilots designed to test and to declare safe, new and repaired aircraft before male pilots in the US Air Force would be allowed to fly them. Twenty-five thousand women applied, 1,830 were accepted, and 1,074 earned their pilot wings. Trainees, already experienced certified pilots each with 500 flying hours, had to complete a seven-month training course of more than three hundred hours of academic studies that included: 24 hours of meteorology, 30 hours of mathematics, 50 hours of physics, 50 hours of maps and navigation, 16 hours of Civil Air Regulations principles of flight, weather, code, instrument flying and communications, 16 hours of aircraft servicing engines and propellers, 24 hours in advanced equipment, 103 hours in physical education and first aid, plus 137 hours in military training.

The women paid their own transportation costs to training sessions, wore uniforms cut for men, were housed in limited spaces on bases where they paid for not only their quarters but the privilege of buying meals in the officer's mess hall. The WASP received no promotions, pay increases, or insurance benefits. Despite this gender abuse, they bravely participated in the war effort participating in dangerous war work.

Aircraft technology was in its infancy, equipment was minimal, radio contact unreliable, there was no radar, no GPS's. Seat belts with chest straps were not yet invented. The WASP flew planes in need of repair in order to determine the repair needed. The safety of the aircraft was unknown until their testing in the air was complete. After a plane had been repaired, a WASP female pilot flew it before an army male pilot flew it.

Virtually every type of aircraft (including early jets) flown by the USAAF men during World War II was flown first by women. These women pilots tested fighters and bombers, they ferried aircraft, flew weather-tracking flights, towed targets through the air during antiaircraft gunnery training, and conducted simulated bombing missions.

Stationed at 120 air bases, they flew more than sixty million miles from aircraft factories to military training bases and to ports of embarkation, delivering more than 12,650 aircraft on which the women pilots then instructed the men. Testing aircraft was an amazing war effort of bravery and ability. But the women were warned to refrain from publicity, literally told to reserve the glamour and glory stories for their frontline brothers.

Julie Stege, remembering her days as a WASP, recalled how the guys "didn't like us at all." They were so humiliated that one of these women could fly a plane. Stege recalled that the guys even wrote their congressmen to get rid of us. The WASP also wrote to Congress to appeal for military status, but they failed in their bid. Congress did not recognize their contributions, their qualifications, or their dedication to the war effort.

Despite gender limitations placed on them, they were zealous. They performed work that male pilots would not risk their lives doing. The mindset, according to Stege was that "If something went wrong, better to lose one of those dames than one of the guys." WASP casualties did occur. Burial boxes and transportation fees to take the body home were at the expense of her family and fellow WASP.

Thirty-eight WASP pilots died in flight-testing accidents. Decades later, investigations suggested that some of the planes had been tampered with and that some of the women pilots died due to sabotage. In the fall of 1944, unemployed male pilots complained that women pilots had taken their jobs. That year, the WASP program was ended.

When the war was over, the women were told to clean up after themselves and buy their own tickets home. They received no veteran benefits. And all records of the WASP were classified and sealed shut. Their contributions to their country were inaccessible to historians for the next thirty-five years. In 1975, Congress was appealed to recognize the WASP as Veterans of World War II entitled to service*men's* benefits. Stege testified before Congress. Ultimately, in 1977, with support of Senator Barry Goldwater (once a ferry pilot), President Jimmy Carter signed legislation granting the WASP full military status.

In 1984, each WASP was awarded the Victory Medal, but not every WASP was alive to accept her award or receive her recognition. Thirty-eight WASP had lost their lives serving their country and more passed away, as time passed. And when they died, there was no furling of the flag, no honor, and no note of heroism for these war heroes of note.

Sources: *Skygirls*, Jenny Laird, director; www.wasp-wwii.org; Charles S. Abell, principal deputy under Secretary of Defense, *Women Pioneering the Future*, Women's War Memorial, Washington, DC, 3/20/03; YouTube: *Mercury 13*—The Secret Astronauts (Part 1); http://www.libertyletters .com/resources/pearl-harbor/women-ferrying-pilots.php.
January 2008

Chapter Thirty-six:
International Women's Day—Why?

~

*B*ecause! Once upon a time, nowhere in the world could women claim to have all the same rights and opportunities as men. Nineteenth century women's oppression and inequality was goading women to become more vocal and active in campaigning for change around the world as well as across the United States.

On July 19, 1848, Elizabeth Cady Stanton and Lucretia Mott organized the Women's Rights Convention in Seneca Falls, New York, to discuss social, civil, and religious conditions as well as the rights of women. It was the first time women's right to vote was presented in a public political forum.

On March 8, 1857, women garment workers in New York City staged a protest against inhumane working conditions and low wages. In the 1880s, a proletarian women's movement concerned with the wages and working conditions of female factory workers, domestic workers, and women in the trades, formed in Germany. Gradually, more of its energy was put into campaigning for women's right to vote.

Women in the United Kingdom were seeking suffrage, too. In 1903, Emmeline Pankhurst founded the Women's Social and Political Union of radical suffragettes. Often the women were brutally beaten by the police, arrested, and jailed at Holloway Prison.

The idea of the International Proletarian Women's Day was conceived in Germany in 1907 when Clara Zetkin suggested that women's demonstrations be held annually on a fixed day all over the world as an expression of international women's solidarity. In 1908, Luise Zietz began to organize such a day.

Also, in 1908, on March 8, fifteen thousand protesters marched through New York City demanding women's rights under the slogan Bread and

Roses. Bread stood for economic security and roses for a better quality of life. The following year, 1909, the Socialist Party of America designated the last Sunday in February as National Women's Day in the United States.

In 1910, when socialist organizations around the world convened in Copenhagen, Zietz formally proposed an international day to mark the strike of garment workers in the United States. Zetkin seconded. More than one hundred women from seventeen countries voiced unanimous agreement. As proposed, International Women's Day was to include the right to vote, but no fixed date of celebration was selected.

International Women's Day was celebrated for the first time in Austria, Denmark, Germany, and Switzerland on March 19, 1911. On that day, more than one million women and men attended International Women's Day rallies campaigning for women's rights to work, to vote, to hold public office, and to end gender discrimination. Forty-one mass meetings were held in Berlin alone and hundreds more in the rest of Germany. Many were filled to overflowing, and men were asked to leave so that more women could be admitted. At every meeting after the speeches, resolutions demanding the vote for women were passed unanimously.

Less than a week later on March 25, the tragic Triangle Shirtwaist Factory Fire in New York City took the lives of more than one hundred forty workingwomen, most of them poor Italian and Jewish immigrants. These workingwomen were locked in sweatshop factory rooms, locked in by the male factory owners, and could not escape. Many jumped out of windows to their death. Many burned to death in the locked factory. This disastrous event drew significant attention to working conditions and labor legislation in the United States that became a focus of subsequent International Women's Day events.

In 1917, in a five-month period, 168 suffragettes were imprisoned in the United States. Alice Paul and fifteen others were arrested in front of the White House and literally thrown into jail. They were handcuffed, beaten, forced to perform hard labor, and placed in solitary confinement. When Britain entered World War I, suffragettes in the United Kingdom suspended their activities to support the war effort. England's suffragettes were released from prison and took on men's jobs.

Russian women held a strike for "bread and peace" in response to the death of more than two million Russian soldiers in the war. After four days, Czar Nicholas II was forced to abdicate, and the provisional government put into place granted women their right to vote. After the war, Britain passed a law in 1918 to allow women over thirty to cast ballots. In the United States, the women's suffrage bill was still in Congress.

In 1921, March 8 was established as the official date of International Women's Day to be celebrated around the globe. However, in the USA, it lay dormant until a new wave of feminism appeared in the 1960s when the day gradually began to be celebrated. Men and women celebrating this day are often asked why in the world would women of the world want to claim an International Women's Day.

The short answer is, because. The long answer is because *nowhere* in the world can women claim to have all the same rights and opportunities as men. And, once upon a time is *now*here. Happy International Women's Day, everywhere, everyone, every year.

Sources: http://en.wikipedia.org/wiki/International_Women's_Day; HBO "Iron Jawed Angels," http://www.internationalwomensday.com/events.asp. March 2008

Chapter Thirty-seven:
Yes, She Can

~

The twelve mile per hour speed limit of the late 1800s soon gave way to auto race speeds that all but drove out women. In 1901, Camille du Gast entered her 20 hp Panhard in a 687-mile race from Paris to Berlin. Du Gast was driven to start last, because her car was half the horsepower of the other 122 male drivers. Still, she finished thirty-third.

For the 1903 Paris to Madrid race, discontent at not competing on equal terms with the men, she entered in an eighty mile per hour De Dietrich. In a field of 207 racers, driving at speeds up to eighty miles per hour, du Gast was in third place and showed women can compete when on equal terms with men. But the race, with rudimentary roads and cars, saw many tragic accidents. Du Gast, well aware of her decision's ramifications, heroically chose to stop to attend to an injured diver whose life, it is said, she saved. Beautiful, with a vivacious personality, she had been very popular. After this rac, she was a role model for women, especially women auto racers.

Mrs. Alice Huyler Ramsey, a Vassar College graduate, founded the first Women's Motoring Club in 1909 and organized the first all-women auto race. Twelve women, two to a car, started in New York, drove to Pennsylvania, and then back two days later. The first, second, and third-place winners drove a Maxwell Runabout, a Lancia Lampo, and a new customized Cadillac respectively.

Six months later, in a 30 hp automobile, Ramsey became the first woman in history to drive solo across country. She made the 3,800-mile trip from New York to San Francisco, but not easily. She was bogged down for twelve rainy days in Iowa, the front wheels of her Maxwell-Briscoe-sponsored open car collapsed when she hit a prairie dog hole in Utah, and eleven sets of fabric tires wore out—but she made it.

Janet Guthrie, had a BSc in physics, was a pilot, a flight instructor, an aerospace engineer, a technical editor, had thirteen years experience on sports car road-racing circuits, and she built and maintained her own race cars. But it was the 1970s and sponsors thought a woman racecar driver was too much of a risk. It was difficult to sell the idea of a female racecar driver to the world and find a sponsor. Eventually, a sponsor took a chance on her, and in 1976, Guthrie became the first woman to compete in a NASCAR super speedway stock car race.

Guthrie recalled that fellow acceptance was slow to come. It took about a year before she could walk through the garage area without having to brace herself, before the attitudes of the crews and drivers started to change. Guthrie said, "That was a nice thing to have happened, very nice." In 1977, she became the first woman to qualify and race in the Indy 500. That same year, she was the first woman and Top Rookie at the Daytona 500. In 1978, she finished ninth at Indy, the best finish ever by a woman, and held that record for twenty-seven years.

The first woman or man to win the National Hot Rod Association Top Fuel championship three times was a woman, Shirley Muldowney ('77, '80, and '82). As the first woman drag racer to exceed 255 miles per hour, Muldowney powered an exceptional racing career that became a 1983 Hollywood movie, *Heart Like a Wheel*. The film was nominated for an Academy Award and a Golden Globe. In the drag racing men's world, where managers aspired that no woman would, should, or (even) could, Muldowney did.

"Boys start racing young, driving go-karts and competing in soapbox derbies. I, on the other hand, went to an all-girl school, took piano lessons, and worked in a steno pool," recalled Lyn St. James. Cars fascinated her, but on her first visit to Indy as a fan, women were not allowed into Gasoline Alley. She started amateur racing in her twenties, but could not afford to race without turning professional. Sponsorship is vital to competing but sponsoring women was not yet vital to male sponsors.

St. James negotiated with a sponsor for three years before being signed and in 1992 she became the Indy 500 Rookie of the Year. "I got big ideas about Indy at an age when most male drivers retire. I drove Indy as the oldest competitor in its history. Now I race vintage cars. My love of the sport—the car, the road and speed—has only increased with age."

In 2005, at the Indianapolis 500, Danica Patrick had a breakthrough fourth-place finish, became Rookie of the Year, and was the first woman to lead a lap at Indy. Only the need to make a pit stop stopped her from a better-than-fourth finish and possibly even winning. She ran out of gas (fuel) but she did not run out. The perennial question then became, "Can she win?" The short answer is "Yes, she can." The long answer is "She did, on April 20, 2008 in the Indy Japan 300."

Sources: Pioneers in the Pit, Journey Gunderson, womenssportsfoundation, 5/05; http://www.roadandtravel.com/celebrities/womensautohistory.html
My First Indy 500, Marion Winik; MORE Dec2005/Jan2006.
May 2008

Chapter Thirty-eight:
Unwelcome Female Nursing Aid

~

*M*en refused medical aid that women offered. They had not asked for help. But news of the abhorrent conditions for the wounded of the Crimean War was leaking out of the country. An estimated eight thousand British soldiers were suffering and dying. But adamant male army doctors did not want female nurses attending them, despite the fact that Secretary of War Sidney Herbert had authorized them.

After the *London Times* published the war causalities, as well as the prejudicial treatment against women's medical service, there was public outcry. The government was forced to relent and in 1853, the British army permitted Florence Nightingale and her group of thirty-eight nurses to enter the main British camp based in Turkey. At the time, Nightingale was an unpaid superintendent at the Institute for the Care of Sick Gentlewomen in Upper Harley Street, London, England.

Nightingale found the health conditions in the army hospital appalling. Medicine was in short supply, hygiene was neglected, and infections, many fatal, were common. Diseases such as typhus, cholera, and dysentery were responsible for more deaths than the fighting. War wounds accounted for only one death in six. Nightingale also found military officers and doctors objected to her views on health reform. They viewed her innovative statistical reports as an attack on their professionalism.

London Times editor, John Delane, championed her cause and exposed details of the British army's brutal treatment of wounded male soldiers and sexist treatment of female nurses. This publicity allowed Nightingale to organize the hospital and improve sanitation conditions that included overcrowding, defective sewers, and poor ventilation. A few months after a sanitary commission flushed out sewers and improved ventilation, death rates sharply declined.

Nightingale developed new techniques of statistical analysis previously unknown. She revolutionized health care, specifically her concept that social phenomena could be objectively measured and expressed in mathematical analyses. Her polar-area diagram, what we all know today as the pie chart graphic with statistics represented proportional to the area of a wedge in a circle, graphically displayed the medical statistics she collected, tabulated, and interpreted.

Her pioneering statistical presentation graphics allowed for organizing and improving all areas of medical procedures. Her Model Hospital Statistical Form allowed hospitals to collect and generate consistent data and statistics. After the war, Herbert led a movement for War Office reform to which Nightingale was a key advisor.

In 1856, Nightingale returned to England a national heroine. She began a campaign to improve nursing and sanitary conditions in military hospitals. She collected and presented data to the Royal Commission on the Health of the Army. She wrote the commission's one thousand-plus page report that included her detailed statistics. Her auspicious report led to a major overhaul of army military care, to the establishment of an army medical school, and it initiated a comprehensive army medical records system. However, Nightingale could not be appointed to the Royal Commission, because she was a woman.

Nightingale's *Notes on Nursing* published in 1860 is the cornerstone of nursing curriculum and considered the classic introduction to nursing. It has been translated into eleven languages and is in print still today. She published more than two hundred books, reports, and pamphlets that continue to be a resource for nurses, health managers, and health planners. Nightingale, literally, organized and developed modern day nursing. She pioneered the development of applied statistics and her feminist writings influenced John Stuart Mill's seminal work, *The Subjection of Women*.

But all the above almost did not happened. As a young girl, Nightingale's wealthy parents disapproved of her desire to become a nurse and preferred she marry. Nursing was associated with working-class women and not considered a suitable profession for well-educated women. Still, Florence, who had rejected many proposals of marriage, preferred a career in medicine.

At St. Bartholomew's Hospital in London, she met Dr. Elizabeth Blackwell, the first woman in the United States to become a doctor. Blackwell had overcome disconcerting gender prejudice to attain her MD. She supported and encouraged Nightingale to persevere. Shortly thereafter, in 1851 at age thirty-one, Florence received her father's permission to train as a nurse. In 1869, Nightingale along with Blackwell opened the Women's Medical College in London.

Infected with disease, most likely during her time in the war zone, she worked in isolation from her room many years hence. In 1895, she became blind and infirm. For the next fifteen years, until her death in 1910, Florence Nightingale required and accepted, unwanted but welcomed full-time nursing care.

Sources: http://www.florence-nightingale.co.uk/index.php; http://www.spartacus.schoolnet.co.uk/REnightingale.htm; http://www.agnesscott.edu/Lriddle/WOMEN/nitegale.htm.
July 2008

Chapter Thirty-nine:
Unbarred Women Paris to Beijing
~

*W*omen were barred from participation in the ancient Olympic Games and in the first modern-day Olympics in Athens in 1896. Women's first Olympic participation began in the 1900 Paris Olympic Games that were part of the Exposition *Universelle Internationale*—the Paris World Fair.

Many competitors did not know if their event was part of the World Exposition or the Olympics. The games were or were not given Olympic status, depending on historic records cited. The French exposition organizers were *laissez-faire* in their organizing and women entered events without opposition. The newly formed all-male International Olympic Committee was against women participating, but these men had little influence in Paris.

It is generally agreed that the first women to compete in the Olympics were Filleaul Brohy and Marie Ohnier of France, who competed against men in the sport of croquet, an Olympic event held only that one year. In tennis, Charlotte Cooper of England, a three time Wimbledon champion, won both the singles and mixed doubles and became the first female Olympic gold medal winner, albeit she did not receive a medal. Medals were first awarded in the 1904 Olympics, and it is written that *women* were the prizes in men's ancient Olympic chariot races. Chicagoan Margaret Ives Abbott was the first American female Olympic champion. However, because of the political confusion over status, Abbott lived and died never knowing of her historic accomplishment.

Tennis, withdrawn after the 1924 games, reappeared in 1984 as a demonstration event won by fifteen-year-old Steffi Graf. When reinstated as an official event in 1988, Graf again won, this time the gold medal.

Archery was included in the 1904 St. Louis Olympic Games where women's boxing happened as a demonstration. Two swimming events and high board diving for women were included in 1912. Fencing for women was added in 1924. Gymnastics appeared as a team sport in 1928, but not as an individual event until 1952. The women's pentathlon event was introduced in the 2000 Sydney Olympics.

Women's and men's individual motocross (BMX) and 10-kilometer marathon in swimming first appeared in the 2008 Beijing Olympics where swimmer Natalie du Toit of South Africa, became the first disabled athlete, female or male, to qualify for the Olympic Games. As well, women's teams in soccer, field hockey, and handball have been increased from ten to twelve teams with women's events added in equestrian and fencing competitions.

The International Olympic Committee (IOC) is committed to gender equity. Only two of twenty-eight Olympic events are not open to women: boxing and baseball. However, the IOC cut girls softball from future Olympics.

And the IOC itself? Well, until 1981, there were no women members only men comprised the initial committee. Women numbered twelve of the 155 members in 2005, and today the IOC member gender balance is an inequitable 15 to140.

Age, as gender, bears an Olympic history of note. The oldest known American woman to have competed in the Summer Olympics is equestrian Kyra Downton who, at age fifty-five, competed in the 1968 games in Mexico City. In Beijing, the oldest American woman to compete is Libby Callahan (fifty-six) in the shooting events. Callahan also competed in the 1992, 1996, and 2004 Olympic games.

After her Olympic tennis championships in 1900, Cooper took off time for family, and then won her fifth Wimbledon singles title in 1908 at the age of thirty-seven and 282 days, an age record that still stands. In 1912, at age forty-one, she continued to be one of the best players and advanced to the Wimbledon finals.

In 2008, at age forty-one, Dara Torres qualified for her fifth Olympics after a six-year hiatus from competition that included the birth of her daughter. This is Torres' second Olympic comeback. After a previous seven-year layoff, she won two relay gold and three individual bronze medals at age thirty-three, the oldest 2000 US Olympic team member.

Torres' swimming successes of the summer add beautiful strokes to a perpetually wet-paint mural of women's sports history. And while Torres may swim alone, swimmingly adding strokes to women's history, she is not alone in the pool of historic Olympic women, young or older, Paris to Beijing.

Source: http://hnn.us/articles/572.html.
August 2008

Chapter Forty:
HERst Castle

~

*J*ulia Morgan was enthralled with mathematics and physics in high school. Upon graduation in 1890, she decided to become an architect. With no architectural schools yet established on the West Coast, she enrolled in the then, all male College of Engineering at the University of California, Berkeley, with the encouragement of her mother and the tolerance of her father. In 1894, she became the first female to graduate Berkeley with a civil engineering degree.

Morgan pursued architectural studies in France at the *École des Beaux-Arts* in Paris per the advice of a professor, but failed the entrance exam twice. She wrote to her professor that she had been failed on purpose because she was female, but that she would try again, "just to show '*les jeunes filles*' are not discouraged." Once accepted, she became the first woman to graduate there, and went on to win medals for her work in mathematics, architecture, and design.

Upon her return to San Francisco in 1902, she became the first woman in California to be licensed as an architect, and helped design several buildings at the University of California, Berkley, including the Hearst Mining Building and the Hearst Greek Theatre. In a man's profession, she started her own firm in 1904, and she was commissioned to build a seventy-two foot tall bell tower at Mills College. An early advocate of building with reinforced concrete, about which she had studied in Paris, she used the product in the tower.

Morgan's office was destroyed, as was most of San Francisco, by the 1906 earthquake, but her seventy-two foot bell tower stood tall. This brought her local acclaim and new commissions, which included rebuilding the earthquake-damaged Fairmont Hotel. Morgan's career was assured and her practice flourished.

One-third of Morgan's clients were women or women's organizations. She designed twenty-eight buildings for the YWCA in California, Utah, and Hawaii, which included a thirteen-building project at the Y's retreat near Monterey that now is a state historical park and conference center.

Morgan never forgot the needs of the single, working-class women aided by the YWCA. Her designs included homelike comforts (i.e., as private kitchenettes and dining areas). She combined beauty with practicality and respected the needs of these women. Some on the YWCA board objected to such details on behalf of these minimum-wage working girls. To Morgan, they were exactly the reason for her details.

In 1919, Morgan had completed the Mission Revival building for the *Los Angeles Examiner*, William Randolph Hearst's flagship newspaper. She was asked by Hearst to design a main building and guesthouses for San Simeon as a tribute to his mother who had died that year, and who Julia had known very well. At the time, Morgan had owned and operated her own firm for twenty years, had already completed some 450 projects, and was much in demand. She accepted his proposal, continued her own business, and worked only weekends on her own time on Hearst's project. Morgan oversaw the work of countless tradesmen and artisans, supervising everything from the overall design to minute details of tile and ornamentation.

Hearst had told her he wanted "something a little different from what other people were doing in California." Little did he know, little seemed not to be part of her or her work. Her design and construction of his villa estate, her weekend job for twenty-eight years, was to become the Hearst Castle.

The Hearst Castle, with 165 rooms, includes a library, a dining room for thirty people, and a private theater. It has fifty-eight bedrooms, fifty-nine bathrooms, eighteen sitting rooms, and two kitchens. The estate has 127 acres of gardens, terraces, indoor and outdoor pools. She designed the Neptune Pool to hang by reinforced-concrete beams in a way that a seismic movement would let it sway but not break.

During her forty-five year career, Morgan designed more than seven hundred homes, churches, hospitals, stores, office, and educational buildings. She employed women, encouraged them in their profession, did not describe herself a feminist, and did not marry. In 1951, Julia Morgan closed her office and retired. She died six years later at the age of eighty-five.

Nearly three hundred linear feet of her architectural drawings are in the library at Cal Poly. The Hearst Castle, now a state historical monument, has attracted millions of visitors since it opened to the public in 1958. California state historical records at Hearst Castle list Julia Morgan as Hearst's private secretary.

Note: In 1972, Sara Boutelle, who taught architectural history at the Brearley School in Manhattan, visited the Hearst Castle for the first time and was horrified to find that the state historical records described Julia Morgan as Hearst's private secretary. Boutelle dedicated the rest of her life to researching and collecting material by and about Julia Morgan.

Sources: *Enterprising Women: 250 Years of American Business,* Virginia G. Drachman; http://www.neh.gov/news/humanities/200609/BeyondSan Simeon.html; http://architecture.about.com/od/greatarchitects/p/julia morgan.htm.
October 2008

Chapter Forty-one:
Wall Street Women

~

*I*n the early days of America, women were considered property of husbands, fathers, or brothers and could not own property separate from their spouses until the mid-1800s. Thus, it was rare for women in the late nineteenth century to be financially independent. Still, it was about that time when women made their first mark on Wall Street.

Origin of the New York Stock Exchange can be traced to May 17, 1792, when twenty-four male stockbrokers signed the Buttonwood Agreement outside 68 Wall Street in New York City. On March 8, 1817, the organization drafted a constitution and renamed itself the "New York Stock & Exchange Board" then dropped "Board" in 1863.

Woodhull, Claflin & Company, the first women-run stockbrokerage firm, opened on Wall Street in 1870. Owners Victoria Woodhull, perhaps best known as the first female to run for the US presidency, and her sister, Tennessee Claflin, are recorded as the first female Wall Street brokers. They prospered through their investments, and the wealthy Cornelius Vanderbilt endorsed their acumen.

The *New York Herald* and other newspapers of the day labeled them as "the Queens of Finance" and "the Bewitching Brokers." In keeping with nineteenth century gender bias customs toward publicly minded, un-chaperoned people who were women, many men's journals linked them to ideas of "sexual immorality and prostitution," and published sexualized images of these two financially savvy women.

Time magazine, March 24, 1924, reports that a Miss Margaret E. McCann, forty-nine, started her own firm dealing in securities but not as a member of any exchange. By 1929, at least twenty-two exchange firms had a woman partner.

In 1930, at a banking symposium sponsored by the Plaza Trust Company of Manhattan, a speaker estimated that 41 percent of US wealth belonged to women and indicated that women seemed to prefer financial advice from other women. Wall Street brokers noted with interest and wondered if the number of women in finance would increase. The firm of Sartorius & Smith, in which Helen Smith Sartorius and Carrie F. Smith were special partners, filed a notice with the New York Stock Exchange that it would dissolve March 31, 1930 and reorganize April 1, 1930, without the women.

Only traders who were men were allowed on the trading floor of the NYSE for 151 years from its inception until 1943, when women traders were allowed to step on this male trading floor to work their trade.

Muriel Siebert began her financial career with a research job in a New York stocks firm in 1954. Siebert changed jobs three times because men in her job earned more than she did. After several inspiring years in finance, her impressive resume did not receive inquires until it was sent out under her initials, M. F., rather than her name, Muriel.

Siebert founded her own firm in 1967 and decided to purchase a seat on the NYSE, but the first nine men she asked to sponsor her turned her down. In an unprecedented Catch 22 move, the exchange insisted she get a bank loan for $300,000 of the $445,000 seat cost, a loan the banks refused unless the exchange made a commitment to her. But Siebert prevailed, and in 1967, she became the first female to hold a seat on the NYSE where she joined 1,365 male members.

Siebert and Company became the nation's first discount broker in 1975. From 1977 to 1982, Siebert served the state of New York as its first female superintendent of banks, or as she says, SOB. Not one New York bank failed during her tenure, albeit bank failures occurred in states nationwide.

In 1990, she created Siebert Entrepreneurial Philanthropic Plan through which she shares half her firm's profits from securities underwriting with charities of the issuers' choices. Through 2006, more than $5 million has been contributed. Since 2005, the Siebert Charitable Stock Donation Program handled more than $39 million of stock donations without commission charges to help charities such as the Red Cross.

Siebert is committed to financial education for all young girls and boys. With nearly one million of her own dollars, she developed a twenty-one-lesson personal finance program for high school students now required in New York City high schools. School boards across the country are reviewing this program.

Many historic women have opened many doors for women in financial careers worldwide. On October 22, 2008 at the Grand Hyatt in New York City, the Deutsche Bank's 14th Annual Women on Wall Street (WoWS) Conference had an attendance of three thousand Wall Street Women. WoW!

Sources: http://query.nytimes.com/gst/fullpage.html?res=9E0CEFD8 143FF936A35754C0A964958260; http://www.theglasshammer.com /news/2008/10/23/wowed-at-the-women-on-wall-street-conference/; http://www.time.com/time/magazine/article/0,9171,738911,00.html; http://en.wikipedia.org/wiki/New_York_Stock_Exchange; https://www .siebertnet.com/html/StartAboutMickie.aspx.
December 2008

Chapter Forty-two:
FLOTUS

~

S
he has a title, an office, and a paid staff accountable to her, but she herself has no pay, no job description, no official job, duties, or power. She is not elected, appointed, or hired. She performs 24/7 service hours of work with a lot of scrutiny in a high profile existence with strong opposition to paid employment outside the White House. Traditionally, she has been a non-working wife. The office of the First Lady of the United States is a branch of the Executive Office of the president.

Martha Washington was never called "First Lady" but rather "Lady Washington." According to legend, Dolley Madison was referred to as first lady in a eulogy delivered by President Zachary Taylor in 1849. However, no written record exists.

The earliest written evidence of the title is found in an 1863 diary entry of William Howard Russell, a Washington correspondent with the *London Times*. Mary C. Ames referred to Lucy Webb Hayes as "the First Lady of the land" in 1877 when reporting on the inauguration of Rutherford B. Hayes. A 1911 Charles Nirdlinger play was titled *The First Lady in the Land*, and by the 1930s the title seemed fixed.

Edith Wilson, the most politically powerful First Lady, has been called the "first female president" of the United States, because she handled government affairs when Woodrow Wilson became partly paralyzed by a stroke.

Anna Eleanor Roosevelt devoted her life to FDR's political career, and she changed the role of First Lady. She traveled, held press conferences, gave lectures and radio broadcasts, and opined in her daily column, "My Day." This most active First Lady was succeeded by the least active of the twentieth century, Bess Truman, who said, "her job was to sit quietly on the podium next to her husband and make sure her hat was on straight."

Mamie Eisenhower set up twenty-seven households in thirty-seven years following Ike's career promotions that brought increased responsibilities for her. An endeared First Lady, she entertained an unprecedented number of foreign government leaders.

Jacqueline Kennedy graduated George Washington University and worked as a photographer before marrying JFK. She defined her major role as First Lady, "to take care of the president." She worked to make the White House a museum of American history and decorative arts, as well as an elegant family residence.

Claudia Taylor "Lady Bird" Johnson devoted herself to her husband's political aspirations. She was active in LBJ's war-on-poverty, specifically the Head Start program. Armed with a BA in arts and journalism, she created a First Lady's Committee for a More Beautiful Capital.

Parentless at an early age, Pat Nixon worked her way through college, graduated cum laude, and then worked as a teacher and a government economist. As First Lady, she promoted volunteer service and traveled alone with relief supplies to earthquake victims in Peru. As personal representative of Richard Milhous, she visited Africa and South America.

Betty Ford trained as a dancer, was a member of Martha Graham's dance group, and taught dance to handicapped children. As First Lady, she openly discussed closeted topics in 1974 such as her breast cancer, her battle against dependency on drugs and alcohol, and controversial issues as the Equal Rights Amendment, which she supported. She helped establish the Betty Ford Center and described the role of First Lady as "much more a 24-hour job than anyone would guess."

Rosalynn Carter, thirteen when her father died, worked with her dressmaker mother to help support the family and raise her younger siblings. As First Lady, she attended cabinet meetings, major briefings, often represented the president at ceremonial occasions, and served as his personal emissary to Latin American countries. She was Honorary Chairperson of the President's Commission on Mental Health and brought national attention to the performing arts.

First Lady Nancy Reagan supported the Foster Grandparent Program and initiated the "just say no" program against drug and alcohol abuse among young people. In 1985, she held a White House conference for first ladies of seventeen countries to focus international attention on this problem. Devoted to the cause of literacy, First Lady Barbara Bush worked for a more literate America.

As Arkansas's First Lady for twelve years, Hillary Clinton parented, practiced law, and performed public service with a focus on children. As the nation's First Lady, Clinton chaired the Task Force on National Health Care Reform. Her weekly newspaper column of her First Lady experiences noted the women, children, and families she encountered globally.

First Lady Laura Bush is Honorary Ambassador for the United Nations Literacy Decade and serves as the international spokesperson for efforts to educate people worldwide, especially women and girls in Afghanistan.

Forty-four white women FLOTUS have held this office. On Inauguration Day, 2009, Barack Obama's *Change* campaign overflows into this office via Harvard lawyer Michelle Obama, the forty-fifth, and the *first* black woman FLOTUS.

Source: http://www.whitehouse.gov/history/firstladies/.
January 2009

Chapter Forty-three:
The Other Babe

~

*B*abe Didrikson-Zaharies (Mildred Ella) as a child, brandished on the gym equipment built by her dad in their backyard. She was a shameless tomboy who excelled in every sport she played: basketball, track, golf, baseball, tennis, swimming, diving, boxing, volleyball, handball, bowling, billiards, skating, and cycling. When asked if there was anything she didn't play, she said, "Yeah, dolls."

She played sandlot baseball with the neighborhood boys and in high school displayed her extraordinary athletic abilities playing girls' basketball. Didrikson said she was nicknamed Babe early in her teens by boys awed at her long-distance homers. Her goal was to be the greatest athlete who ever lived, but few sports' opportunities were open to girls.

The trend in the 1920s was to eliminate interscholastic sports competition for girls due to "undue stress and morbid social influences" upon the female of the species. While girls' intramural athletic games were deemed scholastically suitable, intermural school sports for girls all but disappeared until the 1970s, post Title IX.

Didrikson was neither a declared feminist nor activist for any kind of women's equality. Noticeably she was the antithesis of femininity. She dressed and acted boyish during her youth and on into womanhood. She was simply an athlete. But she was a female.

As a high school senior in 1930, Didrikson was recruited to work for a company, really a ruse as a way for her (women in general) to play basketball on their semiprofessional women's team, the Golden Cyclones. For two years, she led the Cyclones to the finals. In one year, they won the national championship and in both seasons, Didrikson was All-American. Because of her, the company added ten track and field events to the women's sports program. Didrikson represented the company in each, literally, as a one-woman team in each.

At the 1932 Amateur Athletic Union Championships, she placed in seven of the ten events with a first place in five, a tie in one, and fourth in another. She set five world records in a single afternoon, won the team championship, albeit she was the only member of her team. Her thirty points was eight more than the entire twenty-two member second-place team from the University of Illinois (Urbana).

These AAU Championships were the de facto US Olympic Trials and Didrikson qualified for five events in the 1932 Los Angeles Summer Olympics. She would enter in only three. Women, unlike men, were allowed to compete in only three. In all three, she won Olympic medals—two gold and one silver. She won the first women's Olympic javelin event (143 feet, 4 inches) and set a world record in winning the first Olympic eighty-meter hurdles (11.7 seconds). In the high jump, she broke the world record. One sportswriter noted that he never encountered any man who could play as many different games as well as the Babe.

Looking for still another challenge, in 1933 Didrikson turned to golf, which she had played in high school. It would be the sport for which she would become most famous. Though a petite 5' 5", she regularly hit the ball around 250 yards. She won the Texas Women's Amateur golf tournament in 1935, but was denied amateur status by the US Golf Association because her name had appeared in a car advertisement.

Since a professional golf tour for women did *not* exist, she competed in the 1938 men's PGA Los Angeles Open, an arena no other woman would again attempt to enter until Annika Sörenstam (2003), Suzy Whaley (2003), and Michelle Wie (2006), almost six decades later.

In the tournament, Babe was teamed with George Zaharias, a gregarious, well-known professional wrestler and sports promoter who was making a fortune as a stock villain. Though she never had much interest in men, they were married eleven months later. He would become her manager and advisor. But in the years of their marriage, Zaharias lost influence over his wife, and she spent much of her time with Betty Dodd.

Reinstated as an amateur in 1942, she won the 1946 and 1947 US Women's Amateur Golf Championships, the 1947 British Ladies Amateur Golf Championship (the first American to do so), and three Western Opens. She dominated the women's amateur golf circuit winning seventeen straight amateur victories, a feat never equaled by anyone, including Tiger Woods.

She had won every golf title available and turned professional in 1947. Tallying both her amateur and professional victories, Didrikson-Zaharias won eighty-two golf tournaments. She was the leading golfer, male or female, of the 1940s and early 1950s. With twelve other women, she founded the LPGA (Ladies Professional Golf Association) in 1950. In the mid-1950s, cancer curtailed her career and took the life of the other Babe.

Sources: *The Book of Women's Firsts*, Phyllis J. Read and Bernard L. Witlieb; Didrikson was a woman ahead of her time, Larry Schwartz, http://espn .go.com/sportscentury/features/00014147.html; National Women's hall of Fame, www.greatwomen.org; *1001 Things Everyone Should Know About Women's History*, Constance Jones.
May 2009

Chapter Forty-four:
US Supreme Hearts

~

Thirty-nine men convened in Philadelphia in 1787 to frame the US Constitution. In it, they defined the Supreme Court. Their Constitution is a living document, interpreted by judges, often with decisions that traverse. The Supreme Court is the highest court from which there is no appeal. Its justices are appointed for life by the president. Its decisions are the laws of the land that govern men and women. In the 1930s, Chief Justice Charles Hughes stated, "We are under a Constitution but the Constitution is what the Judges say it is."

In his book, *Man & Wife in America: A History,* Hendrik Hartog writes how patriarchy and misogyny were present in the legal culture as well as in the words and worlds of judges. He notes that after the framing of the Constitution, for more than 160 years, all the public officials and the authoritative legal voices were all male—judges, legislators, juries, treatise writers—all of them. As late as the 1950s, Hartog writes that women were a minuscule fraction of American lawmakers. Questions arose if gender and/or race had entered into legal decisions and statements.

In 1952, prior to his appointment to the Supreme Court, in a memo during deliberations that led to the *Brown v. Board of Education* (*) decision, William Rehnquist, a white male wrote, "To the argument ... that a majority may not deprive a minority of its constitutional right, the answer must be made that while this is sound in theory, in the long run it is the majority who will determine what the constitutional rights of the minorities are." Women are the majority (51 percent), but systemically are a minority in economic, social, and political decisions and seats of decision-making powers.

During America's first 192 years, not one female was a judge on the Supreme Court defining and deciding what is law. All law making-and-law-breaking Supreme Court decisions were decided by "men only" until Sandra Day O'Connor became the 102nd and first woman Supreme Court Justice in 1981. O'Connor was the solo woman on the court for eleven years until Ruth Bader Ginsburg became the 107th and second woman Supreme Court Justice in 1993.

Rather than being strictly liberal or conservative, O'Connor was both and neither, often the swing vote. During oral arguments about a widow denied use of her property, most of the justices focused on legal precedents. O'Connor said, "Why not give this poor, elderly woman the right to go to court?" In a student-on-student case of a fifth grade girl sexually harassed by a boy, O'Connor rejected the argument that this decision would teach "little Johnny" the wrong lesson about federalism but argued, it would ensure that "little Mary may attend class."

Ginsburg's philosophy of equal treatment for women and *men* who do not conform to society's gender-based stereotypes, allows men to assume traditional female roles. (i.e., her victory in the case of a young widower whose wife had died in childbirth and because of his gender was ineligible to receive Social Security benefits to enable him to work part-time and stay home to care for his baby.) In the famous 1991 Supreme Court decision to allow women to attend the all-male Virginia Military Institute, Ginsburg reformulated the question before the court, not whether a female can be admitted to the all-male VMI, but whether the government can constitutionally deny admittance to a qualified applicant because of gender.

In America's 222-year history, a meager thirteen years of law making and breaking Supreme Court decisions decided upon by two women and seven men ended and reversed in 2005 when O'Connor retired and was replaced by a male. That same year, after Chief Justice Rehnquist died, another male was appointed, leaving Ginsburg the solo female voice on the court, a voice challenged by cancer and aging.

In 2001, in a speech during a conference discussing Latino and Latina presence in the judiciary, responding to the saying that "a wise old man and wise old woman will reach the same conclusion in deciding cases," Judge Sonia Sotomayor stated, "First, there can never be a universal definition of wise. Second, I would hope that a wise Latina woman with the richness of her experiences would more often than not reach a better conclusion than a white male who hasn't lived that life." Again, questions arose if gender and/or race had entered into legal decisions and statements.

In 2005 in his senate vote against confirming Supreme Court Chief Justice John Roberts, in regard to the judicial decision-making process, then-senator Barack Obama stated that where, "... constitutional text will not be directly on point ... Legal process alone will not lead you to a rule of decision ... in those difficult cases, the critical ingredient is supplied by what is in the judge's heart." To date, the 110 Supreme Court justices' hearts have been in 108 men and two women.

In 2009, to replace retiring Supreme Court Justice David Souter, President Obama nominated Judge Sotomayor to become the 111th and third female, US Supreme heart.

(*) The 1954 *Brown v. Board of Education* Supreme Court decision, stating separate but equal was not legal, overturned the ruling of the 1896 *Plessy v. Ferguson* Supreme Court decision stating separate but equal was legal.
July 2009

Chapter Forty-five:
No small Step for Women
~~

Nine years before 1969, when man first stepped on the moon, thirteen women tested to qualify for America's astronaut training program. These thirteen pilots did qualify in all but one category, that of gender. In general, women weighed less, ate less, and used less oxygen, (all reducing the cargo weight), and thus would need less booster power (expensive fuel) to propel them into space than the seven men who were propelled. As their pilot stats and stories avow, thirteen women pilots, now known as the *Mercury 13*, were as well, if not better qualified than the seven men pilots who would be America's first astronauts known as the *Mercury 7*.

The physical-fitness testing regimen to select US astronauts was in part developed by Dr. William Randolph Lovelace. He and renowned pilot Jacqueline Cochran—the first American woman to break the sound barrier, founder of the WASP, and friend of Amelia Earhart—wanted to prove that women were equally qualified to be astronauts. Thus, in 1960, Lovelace privately invited pilot Geraldyn "Jerrie" Cobb to undergo the tests.

Cobb got her private pilot's license at seventeen, her commercial license at eighteen, and her flight instructor's rating shortly thereafter. She decided upon a career in aviation as a pilot, all but an impossible female dream in the 1950s. Still, Cobb went on to fly all types of aircraft worldwide including military aircraft and four-engine bombers to France. She was perhaps the most experienced high-performance propeller aircraft pilot of her day, male or female. She earned world records for speed, altitude, and distance, and in 1960, she had ten thousand flying hours compared to John Glenn's five thousand flying hours.

After Cobb passed the testing and became the first American woman to qualify for astronaut training, she and Dr. Lovelace publicly announced her test results at a news conference in Stockholm. Reporters from all over the world called. Cobb said they asked, "What were my measurements, my favorite color, and why wasn't I married?" It has been written that Dr. Lovelace may have been ahead of his time in 1960 concerning woman's place in space and in society. Perhaps. Albeit his tests would determine the pilots' best qualified sans any gender bias.

Cobb, Lovelace, and Cochran, began recruiting women pilots to test. Many were recruited through Ninety-Nines, Inc., a women pilot's organization. Twenty-five of America's top women pilots were selected. Secretly and independent of one another, they underwent four days of physical and psychological testing identical to the male pilots.

Lovelace tested their reflexes using electric shock. He shot ice water in their ears to freeze the inner ear and induce vertigo. He put them in an isolation tank filled with water to see how long they could endure before hallucinating. Some outperformed their male counterparts. Most men lasted two to three hours before they started hallucinating. Cobb lasted nine hours and forty minutes. Thirteen experienced female pilots, several with more flight hours than the *Mercury 7* men, passed the tests but did not and could not pass the male criterion.

In the early days of space program planning, President Dwight David Eisenhower wanted only jet test pilots considered. This eliminated all women and minorities. All jet test pilots were white males and NASA maintained this gender bias requirement.

Lyndon Baines Johnson forwarded the legislation that created NASA and was now head of the President's Space Council. Liz Carpenter, his press representative, drafted a letter for Johnson's signature to NASA's James Webb simply inquiring about spaceflight gender qualifications, thinking it would be good press for LBJ to show support for the women. Instead of affixing his signature, Johnson scrawled, "Let's Stop This Now!"

The summer of 1961, just before leaving for the next phase of training at the Naval Aviation Center in Pensacola, Florida, the thirteen women pilots who became known as the *Mercury 13*—Geraldyn "Jerrie" Cobb, Myrtle "K" Thompson Cagle, Jan Dietrich, Marion Dietrich, Mary Wallace "Wally" Funk, Jane "Janey" Briggs Hart, Jean Hixson, Gene Nora

Stumbough Jessen, Irene Leverton, Sarah Lee Gorelick Ratley, Bernice "B" Steadman, Geraldine "Jerri" Sloan Truhill, and Rhea Allison Hurrle Woltman—received telegrams telling them not to come, their project had been canceled. They had given up their jobs and careers, left their parents, husbands, and children all for the chance to go to space. NASA unabashedly decided against including women in the program.

Cobb met with Vice President Johnson who told her, "Jerrie, if we let you or other women into the space program, we'd have to let blacks in, we'd have to let Mexican-Americans in, we'd have to let every minority in, and we just can't do it." Two years later, in 1963, the Soviet Union sent the first woman into space.

Twenty years later in 1983, Sally Ride became the first female US astronaut in space. Dr. Mae Jemison became the first black female (fifth black) US astronaut in 1988. At the space shuttle launch, February 1995, the seven living *Mercury 13* women were guests of astronaut Lieutenant Colonel Eileen Collins. These women pilots watched as Collins stepped into *Columbia* and soared into space as the first female pilot of a space shuttle: A giant leap for mankind and no small step for women.

Sources: *The Mercury 13*, Martha Ackmann; http://space.about.com/od /spaceexplorationhistory/a/mercury13.htm.
August 2009

Chapter Forty-six:
The Lady and The Law School

~

*I*n the 1800s, men studied law under the supervision of a practicing attorney or attended law school. Men did not admit women to their law schools, albeit some male lawyers did accept women to study law in their private practices.

In 1855, Myra Bradwell began her law studies under a practicing attorney, her husband, and apprenticed in his law practice, as well.

In 1861, Bradwell coauthored the Illinois Married Women's Property Act.

In 1868, Bradwell founded the *Chicago Legal News*.

In 1869, Lemma Barkeloo became the first woman in America admitted to law school at Washington University in St. Louis.

In 1870, Ada Kepley became the first woman in America to graduate with a formal law degree from Union College of Law, now Northwestern University in Chicago.

In 1870, the US census notes five women lawyers.

In 1873, Bradwell was denied access to the Illinois State Bar, because she was a woman, though she had passed the bar exam with honors. The US Supreme Court upheld the Illinois Supreme Court decision.

In 1886, Alice R. Jordon Blake, using only her initials, was accepted at Yale Law School. Her gender discovered, she argued, "There isn't a thing in your catalogue that bars women." That year, Yale included the words, "It is to be understood that the courses of instruction are open to the male sex only." No other woman would graduate Yale Law School for seventy-four years.

In 1898, African-American attorney Lutie A. Lytle became the first female law professor in the world when she joined the faculty of Central Tennessee College of Law.

In 1898, Ellen Spencer Mussey and Emma Gillett founded Washington College of Law in the District of Columbia as coed specifically for women rejected by law schools. It is now American University.

In 1900, the US census notes 1,010 women lawyers.

In 1919, Yale Law School admits women students.

In 1919, Barbara Armstrong became the first woman appointed to a tenure-track position at an accredited law school, the University of California at Berkeley.

In 1938, Pauli Murray's rejection letter from the University of North Carolina Law School read, "Members of your race are not admitted to the university." At Howard University Law School, where she was the only female in her class, her professor said in his opening remarks on the first day that he really did not know why women came to law school, but since they were there, the men would have to put up with them. Murray graduated first in her class.

In 1944, Murray's rejection letter for an advanced degree program at Harvard Law School read, "Your picture and the salutation on your college transcript indicate that you are not of the sex entitled to be admitted to Harvard Law School."

In 1946, Sandra Day O'Connor, well aware she might not be accepted because she was a woman, was admitted to Stanford. She completed a dual-degree, seven-year program in six years receiving a bachelor's in economics in 1950 and a law degree in 1952. She graduated third in her class, but could not get a job as a lawyer because of her gender. She was offered a position as a legal secretary, which did not match her education, training, or ability. She did not accept the position.

In 1948, Patsy Mink, with dual bachelor's degrees in zoology and chemistry, applied to twenty medical schools. None accepted women. Judging the judicial process was needed to adjudicate this gender injustice, Mink decided to attend law school. She applied to the University of Chicago Law School that had admitted women from its inception in 1902 and obtained her JD in 1951, the only woman in her graduating class. Unable to find employment in the legal field, she did odd jobs and worked in the law school's library before starting her own law firm.

In 1950, Harvard Law School opened to women and fourteen joined the class of 520 men. They were invited to speak only on Ladies Day, a single class that met once each month, they were allowed to eat in the graduate cafeteria, and one ladies room was added in the basement of Austin Hall. Dorms opened to women eight years later.

In 1954, Ruth Bader Ginsburg entered Harvard Law School as one of nine women in a class of more than five hundred. Of these women, Dean Erwin Griswold asked what it felt like to occupy places that could have gone to deserving men. When her husband joined a law firm in New York Ginsburg transferred to Columbia Law School where in 1959 she graduated first in her class. No law firm offered her a job.

In 1960, Supreme Court Justice Felix Frankfurter was asked to consider hiring Ginsburg as one of his law clerks. He refused to interview her acknowledging he was just not ready to hire a woman. Ginsburg taught at Rutgers and Columbia.

In 1960, the US census notes seven thousand women lawyers.

In the 1960s, during her early days of law school at Northwestern University, current US House Representative Judy Biggert (R-Illinois) said she was told that she was a student by mistake—a man should have been in her seat.

In 1965, Mink became the first female minority elected to the US House of Representatives (D-Hawaii).

In 1969, the first Women and the Law courses in the country were taught at NYU Law School in the fall semester and at Yale the following spring semester.

In 1970, the US census notes thirteen thousand women lawyers.

In 1970, Ginsburg cofounded the "Women's Rights Law Reporter," the first law journal to focus exclusively on women's rights.

In 1972, Mink coauthored Title IX with US House Representative Edith Green (D-Oregon).

In 1974, "Sex-Based Discrimination," coauthored by Ginsburg, Kenneth M. Davidson, and Herma Hill Kay, was published as the first law school casebook addressing the topic.

In 1976, Sonia Sotomayor entered Yale Law School on a scholarship. A prominent law firm suggested she was only at Yale via affirmative action. She sued and the firm apologized.

In 1978, *Duren v. Missouri*, Ginsburg argued that optional jury duty was a message that women's service was unnecessary to important government functions. At the end of Ginsburg's oral presentation then Associate Justice William Rehnquist asked Ginsburg, "You won't settle for putting Susan B. Anthony on the new dollar, then?"

In 1980, the US census notes sixty-two thousand women lawyers.

In 1981, O'Connor became the 102nd, first female, US Supreme Court Justice (101 men).

In 1993, Ginsburg became the 107th, second female, US Supreme Court Justice (105 men).

In 2009, Sotomayor became the 111th, third female, US Supreme Court Justice (108 men).

In 2009, the US census notes 333,000 women lawyers.

Incalculable evidence notes a history of law linked to The Lady & The Law School.

Sources: *Women in Law*, Cynthia Fuchs Epstein; *The Nine: Inside The Secret World of the Supreme Court*, Jeffrey Toobin; *Law school: Legal education in America from the 1850s to the 1980s*, Robert Stevens; www.politico.com/news/stories/0909/27152.html,http://www.washlaw.edu/subject/legal.history.html A Timeline of Women's Legal History by Professor Cunnea. October 2009

Chapter Forty-seven:
Wife/Copilot

~

*A*nne Morrow Lindbergh was critical to the success of Charles Lindbergh's flights. She was his radio operator, navigator, and copilot. After his New York to Paris solo flight, May 1927, Lucky Lindy had his choice of copilots. He chose Miss Anne Morrow.

They met that December when he flew the *Spirit of St. Louis* to Mexico at the invitation of US Ambassador, Dwight Morrow, Anne's father. Charles was ready to move on from stunt flying, barnstorming, and competitive racing to serious flight explorations and he wanted to marry. And he wanted to marry a healthy woman who liked flying, because he wanted his wife to be his flying companion on expeditions he planned to make. He set his sights on Anne whom he invited to go flying. If all went well in the air as he planned—well. He let her experience the controls and logged in fifty-five minutes as her first flight training. When she told him that night that she wanted to learn to fly, he smiled.

They married in May 1929, honeymooned alone-together for three weeks roughing it on a thirty-eight-foot motorboat eating canned goods and drinking ginger ale. The honeymoon Charles planned previewed the couple's flight adventures to come and provided a peek at his wife in such a situation, a situation Anne enjoyed quiet well.

He began her formal flight training immediately with flight aerobatics and landings, pitch angles, bank angles, navigation, calculating arrival based on ground speed, etc. The following year she would fly more than thirty thousand miles. She was the relief pilot on all the Lindbergh expeditions. Together they pioneered aerial photography and archaeological exploration of the Mayan ruins in the Yucatan. Together they flew in a record-breaking flight Los Angeles to New York, during which seven-month pregnant Anne served as navigator and copilot. She then copiloted three more flights for Charles before birthing their son on June 22, 1930.

Anne completed her training and resumed flying with Charles the first week of August. Together they explored Central and South America. Together they learned celestial navigation for their flight around the world. The final weeks before that flight, Charles trained her hard to earn licenses both to fly and to operate the airborne radio. Anne, anxious about satisfying Charles' expectations, passed her flight tests on May 28, 1931.

Distraught about leaving her baby, her role as dutiful wife was in conflict with her role as mother. Still, together she and Charles took off from New York on July 27 for their survey flight over vast tundra, virgin territory, away from civilization, to circumvent the world and chart air routes. On a stop in Canada, a pilot noted their rugged route and commented that he would not take his wife over that terrain. Charles replied, "You must remember that she is crew." Anne wondered if she had reached the point of equal footing with men, her man, not just a wife, but also a copilot. Then, upon landing in Japan after 7,132 miles, the press wrote that Anne, helping Charles with his kimono, possessed the virtues of an attentive wife.

In China, where the Yangtze had overflowed killing 3.7 million people and leaving thirty million homeless, together they did relief work. Anne piloted over four and one half hours one day, and over seven the next, flying low and dexterous so Charles could chart and photograph flooded areas. Learning that Anne's father had died, together they made plans to return home. Two and one half months after their takeoff in New York, together they had charted ten thousand miles for future flight routes.

In May 1932, their young son was kidnapped and killed; Anne was pregnant and gave birth to their second son Jon in August. One year later, though torn to leave Jon, together she and Charles left on an Atlantic survey flight, a thirty thousand mile exploration to four continents over a five-month period.

Women began to view Anne as a role model. She was the first woman to fly across the South Atlantic, the first woman and tenth American to earn a first class glider pilot's license. She was the first woman to earn the Veteran Wireless Operators Association's gold medal, and the third woman pilot awarded an honorary membership in the National Aeronautic Association of the USA. The National Geographic Society awarded her, the first woman, and only the tenth person in the half century of its existence, the Hubbard Medal. The United States Flag Association presented her their Cross of Honor. As the first woman to fly forty thousand miles of uncharted sky during 1931–33, the International League of Aviators awarded her the Harmon National Trophy as America's champion aviatrix for 1933, because she had "done most to advance aviation during the year." In 1934, her alma mater Smith College started a young women's flying club.

Anne gave birth to their third son Land in 1937. In 1938, she reluctantly went along with Charles' decision to move them from their home at Long Barn that Anne loved, to an isolated island he had purchased off the Brittany coast of France and into an 1865 stone house, which needed renovation, lacked heat, plumbing, electricity, and indoor toilets. That year, the American embassy in London asked Charles to survey Russia's aviation industry. He wanted his wife along. Anne did not wish to leave their children, but felt she needed to go with her husband. It proved to be their last extended flight together. When her license expired, she chose not to renew it and to close this chapter in her life.

Together Charles and Anne would have three more children, Anne (1940), Scott (1942), and Reeve (1945). In 1946, together they purchased a home in Connecticut. Together they authored many books. Their youngest daughter Reeve said they wrote not in collaboration but in mutual awareness and with mutual support. Of Anne's fourteen books, *A Gift from the Sea* sold more than three million copies and is printed in forty-five languages. Charles' *Spirit of St. Louis* earned him a Pulitzer Prize.

Charles continued his aeronautic work and was away from Anne and the children most of the last two decades of his life. During this period, he was silent about his whereabouts and she remained subservient and devoted. She discovered her independence, grew her confidence, and became head of her household.

In the late 1960s, they began to travel again together. In 1974, with Anne by his side, Charles died of cancer. In 2001, at age ninety-four and frail, surrounded by family and friends, Anne died peacefully.

In 2003, it became public that Charles had seven children in Europe conceived and birthed by three women other than his wife and copilot Anne Morrow Lindbergh and that from his deathbed, he wrote a letter to each of the other three women requesting "utmost secrecy."

Sources: *Anne Morrow Lindbergh: First Lady of the Air,* Kathleen C. Winters; "Secrets and Lives," MORE, March 2008, Reeve Lindbergh; *Under A Wing: A Memoir,* Reeve Lindbergh; *Das Doppelleben des Charles A. Lindbergh (The Double Life of Charles A Lindbergh),* Rudolf Schroeck. November 2009

Chapter Forty-eight:
Her Un-Silent Season

~

S *ilent Spring* written by Rachel Carson in 1962 gave genesis to the
environmental movement. It created public awareness to the affect
and potential dangers of chemical use on the entire ecosystem, specifically
that of DDT whose benefits were well known, albeit its dangers were not.

As an author and aquatic biologist with the US Bureau of Fisheries,
Carson had been writing about conservation and nature for the bureau,
and for newspapers and magazines since 1929. By1962, she had authored
three books, *Under the Sea-Wind* (1941), *The Sea Around Us* (1951), and
The Edge of the Sea (1956). *The Sea Around Us* was on the best-seller list for
eighty-six weeks and translated in thirty-two languages.

Nature and writing was a part of Carson since her childhood on a farm
near the Allegheny River where at the age of ten, a children's magazine
published her work. In 1925, she entered Pennsylvania College for Women
as an English major, changed majors and graduated magna cum laude with
a degree in biology. After a summer fellowship at the Marine Biological
Laboratory in Massachusetts, Carson entered John Hopkins University on
a scholarship awarded to her for her graduate work and earned her master's
in zoology in 1932 amazing accomplishments for a woman then. Plans to
pursue her doctorate were not realized due to the unexpected death of her
father and her need to work and care for her aging mother.

Though a woman in a predominately man's world of fish and fowl,
Carson's proficiency in writing and biology earned her a part-time position
with the US Bureau of Fisheries to write a series of fifty-two educational
weekly radio broadcasts focused on aquatic life. She also wrote newspaper
and magazine articles on marine life in the Chesapeake Bay. In 1936,
having outscored all her *fellow* civil service exam applicants, Carson became

the second woman to be hired by the bureau for a full-time professional position as a junior aquatic biologist. She was to analyze and report field data on fish populations, write brochures for the public, and continue writing to respected magazines and newspapers as *The Baltimore Sun*.

One essay she wrote for the *Atlantic Monthly* was assessed by her supervisor to be, "too good" for a magazine. It became her first book. At the bureau, now Fish and Wildlife Service, Carson was promoted to aquatic biologist in 1943, then to assistant editor, and then editor-in-chief of all publications. During World War II, she participated in a program investigating undersea sounds, life, and terrain, designed to assist the navy in developing techniques and equipment for submarine detection.

In 1945, when jobs and federal funds focused on technical science, specifically military funding to develop the atomic bomb, and not funding on fish and wildlife, Carson became aware of DDT, a new synthetic pesticide known as the insect bomb. Tests for safety and ecological effects of DDT were just beginning.

DDT's use worldwide increased exponentially after World War II primarily because of its effectiveness against the mosquito that spreads malaria and lice that carry typhus. It appeared the ideal insecticide, cheap and of relatively low toxicity to mammals. However, in the late 1940s, problems related to its extensive use began to appear. Many insects developed resistance, and it showed a high toxicity toward fish. Since abnormalities show up first in fish and wildlife, biologists were the first to see any impending danger. DDT scrutiny was one of Carson's writing interests but not one her editors preferred, or preferred to publish.

The success of her second book in 1952 enabled Carson to resign and devote her time to writing. She published her third book and closely followed federal USDA plans for widespread pesticide spraying programs, specifically the program to eradicate fire ants. She also began research on the ecology and organisms of the Atlantic shore. For the remainder of her life, the dangers of pesticide overuse on the environment would be her focus.

Evidence of DDT poisoning the environment increased with reports of poisonings of birds, fish, and small game. At Michigan State University, annual DDT spraying of elms to control the beetle that spreads Dutch elm disease began in 1954. After about a year, no robins were seen on campus. Earthworms feeding on elm leaves accumulated DDT and when a level toxic to robins was reached, robins that ate those worms died—as did robins that came two years after spraying had been discontinued. Mud in the bottom of Green Bay, an arm of Lake Michigan, was found to contain DDT. The billions of crustaceans living in the mud absorbed it in their bodies as did fish feeding on the crustaceans and herring gulls feeding on the fish.

By the late 1950s, Carson and others found DDT in the brains of prematurely dead bald eagles and proffered DDT in the food chain was largely responsible. Oceanic food chains were similarly contaminated. Ocean currents were spreading DDT residues to remote corners of the earth. It was also detected in Antarctic snow.

In January 1958, Carson's friend Olga Owens Huckins described to her the deadly effect of DDT spraying for mosquitoes over the Huckinses' private two-acre bird sanctuary in Massachusetts. Carson was visiting when the spraying plane flew over. The next morning, she saw crayfish and crabs dead or staggering, their nervous systems destroyed. The Huckins beseeched her to write about this.

Carson biologically documented a need for DDT to be responsibly managed and sprayed. In 1959, she wrote a letter published in *The Washington Post* that attributed the recent decline in bird populations—in her words, the "silencing of birds"—to pesticide overuse.

After an unsuccessful legal suit by landowners in New York State to restrict DDT use in the state, the editor of *The New Yorker* petitioned Carson to write an article about it. It became her next book, *Silent Spring*.

Sources: http://www.americanheritage.com/articles/magazine/ah/1971/2/1971_2_44.shtml http://www.fws.gov/northeast/rachelcarson/carsonbio.html.
January 2010

Chapter Forty-nine:
Her March-His Moment

~

*I*da B. Wells began the antilynching campaign. Rosa Parks sat on a bus. Jo Ann Robinson initiated the Montgomery bus boycott. Pauli Murray organized the first restaurant sit-in. Daisy Bates desegregated schools in Little Rock. Mary White Ovington started the NAACP. Fannie Lou Hamer desegregated the Democratic National Convention, and in April 1963, Coretta Scott King suggested a march on Washington, DC. Women were active in the civil rights movement.

Women, active in the civil rights movement, were not allowed to march, individually or as wives with their husbands, in the August 1963 Great March on Washington, DC. These women activists also were not allowed to be with the men of the civil rights movement to meet President John F. Kennedy at the White House after that march in which 250,000 men and women participated.

Coretta Scott began her education in 1933 in a one-room rural school in Alabama and graduated high school as her class valedictorian. She then attended and graduated from Antioch College in Ohio as a music and education major and enrolled in the New England Conservatory of Music in Boston. During her senior year of studies preparing for a career in music education, she married and graduated the summer of 1954 as the wife of Pastor Martin Luther King, Jr. In November 1955, she gave birth to their first child.

Three weeks later, on December 1, Rosa Parks was arrested. That night Jo Ann Robinson printed (mimeographed) 52,500 leaflets calling for a bus boycott in Montgomery. On December 5, the Montgomery Improvement Association met and named Martin Luther King, Jr., its president as the women in the MIA looked on. On January 30, 1956, the King parsonage was bombed.

During the following seven years, Coretta gave birth to their next three children and actively worked for racial justice in the shadow of Martin. She joined the Women's International League for Peace and Freedom (the organization founded by Jane Addams and the main reason Addams was awarded the Nobel Peace Prize), and she began speaking publicly, specifically to youth and women's groups.

In the sixties, Coretta served as a delegate for the Women's Strike for Peace Conference in Geneva, Switzerland. She participated in the Selma to Montgomery March and the James Meredith Civil Rights March Against Fear in Mississippi. She spoke at a peace rally in Madison Square Garden in New York City, and served as a delegate to the White House Conference "To Fulfill These Rights." She participated in the Women's Peace Brigade March in Washington, DC led by Jeannette Rankin, the first woman elected to the US Congress and the only member of Congress to vote no against America's entry into two world wars.

After Martin's death in 1968, Coretta established his memorial fund, began plans for an annual Martin Luther King, Jr., birthday celebration, and initiated plans to form the King Center. She became the first woman to speak at a Harvard graduation, and she received an honorary doctorate from Boston University.

In the 1970s, Coretta was appointed pubic delegate to the United Nations, co-founded the Black Leadership Forum and the Black Leadership Roundtable, and was appointed Deputy Chair for the White House Conference on Families.

In the 1980s, she addressed the Hispanic Leadership Conference in Houston; spoke at two Democratic National Conventions, at the International Day of Solidarity with South Africa Rally, at a disarmament rally in Bonn, Germany, and at the World Peace March in 1982, which called on the United Nations for a special session on disarmament.

That decade she also helped plan the twentieth anniversary of the March on Washington, met with Indira Gandhi, and observed President Ronald Reagan sign a bill to establish the birthday of Martin Luther King, Jr., as a federal holiday. She endorsed the Women's Peace Platform and presented it to the United Nations, participated in the National March for

Housing Now in Washington, DC where she met with President George H. W. Bush and Vice-President Dan Quayle.

In the 1990s, she convened the Soviet-American Women's Summit, participated in the twenty-fifth anniversary of the Selma to Montgomery March, spoke out against the bombing of Iraq, called for a march on Washington to commemorate the thirtieth anniversary of Martin's "I Have a Dream" speech, and hosted a roundtable discussion on nonviolence that included Desmond Tutu and Andrew Young.

In April of 2000, she celebrated her seventy-fifth birthday. In 2005, she became ill, suffered a major stroke, and was diagnosed with ovarian cancer.

Coretta Scott King, the woman who (because she was a woman) could not officially march in the historic 1963 Great March on Washington DC, which she proposed, marched to the beat of her own drum for half a century until January 30, 2006 when her heart beat stopped.

Source: *Coretta Scott King: A Biography*, Laura T. McCarty.
February 2010

Chapter Fifty:
Her Bly-Line
～

*E*lizabeth Jane Cochran was a bold, early nineteenth century reporter. She was born in 1864 in Armstrong County, Pennsylvania, forty miles northeast of Pittsburgh. Her father a wealthy associate justice, died when she was just six years old. When she was nine, her mother remarried but divorced five years later. Elizabeth Jane, fourteen, was called to testify against her drunken, violent stepfather. She left boarding school after one year to move with her family to Pittsburgh and added an *e* to her surname for a touch of sophistication.

As a teen, a sexist column she read in the *Pittsburgh Dispatch* prompted a fiery rebuttal to the editor. Impressed with her spirit, he asked her to join the editorial staff. Since it was considered improper at the time for women to write publicly under their own names, he requested she choose a pseudonym. Cochrane chose "Nellie Bly" from a song by Stephen Foster.

Bly's writing focused on the plight of working women. Her series of investigative reports on female factory workers exposed heinous conditions and got her moved to the women's pages to cover fashion, society, and gardening. She followed that move with one of her own at age twenty-two when she chose to go to Mexico as a foreign correspondent for the *Dispatch* to report on the lives and customs of the Mexican people. Her reports led to her first book, *Six Months in Mexico.*

One of her reports protested the incarceration of a local journalist who had been imprisoned for criticizing the Mexican government under the dictatorship of Porfirio Díaz. Threatened with arrest for this report, she wisely left the country. Back in the states, free of any censorship and fear of her own incarceration, she continued to denounce Díaz for suppressing the Mexican people and controlling the press.

Back at the *Dispatch*, she once again was assigned to social reporting. This time, she left the newspaper as well as Pittsburgh and moved to New York. Twenty-three and broke, Bly talked her way into the offices of the *New York World*, a Joseph Pulitzer newspaper, and landed an assignment in 1887 to investigate rumors of brutality and neglect at the Women's Lunatic Asylum on Blackwell's Island. To get the assignment she agreed to feign insanity and get committed.

She studied female behaviors labeled as lunacy and practiced deranged expressions in front of a mirror. She checked into a working-class boardinghouse and began behaving bizarrely. She refused to go to bed, cowered, and told the boarders they looked crazy and that she was afraid of them. The boarders, themselves afraid of her, agreed *she* was the crazy one and summoned the police to haul her away.

When brought before a judge, she faked amnesia. The judge had her examined by doctors who declared her insane, and the court committed her to Blackwell. The *New York Sun* and the *New York Times* reported on this "mysterious waif" with the "wild, hunted look in her eyes," and her desperate outcry, "I can't remember! I can't remember!"

Once committed, she went to work. She found the food inedible— gruel broth, spoiled meat, and bread that was little more than dried dough. She experienced conditions first hand for ten days until the *New York World* had her released to begin reporting.

She described how patients were mistreated and made to sit on straight-back benches from 6:00 a.m. to 8:00 p.m., during which time they were not allowed to talk. They were not given any reading material. They received no news of the outside world. (*) Two months of this, she reported, would make any sane person insane. Her reports launched a grand jury investigation and became her famous book, *Ten Days in a Madhouse*.

Bly next suggested to her editor a trip around the world, derisively miming Jules Verne's 1888 book, *Around the World in Eighty Days*. Her editor sent her in 1889. She returned in seventy-two days, six hours, eleven minutes and fourteen seconds—a new world record. Of course, she reported this. As she traveled the world by steamship, railroad, rickshaw, and sampan, she demonstrated female independence from men and that travel could be safe and fun for single women.

Back home, Bly continued to relentlessly report on poor conditions around the country and the world. In 1922, Elizabeth Jane Cochrane died of pneumonia at age fifty-seven.

(*) See Charlotte Perkins Gilman, "The Yellow Wallpaper."

March is Women's History Month. For information and ways to celebrate, visit www.nwhp.org or womenshistorymonth.gov.
March 2010

Chapter Fifty-one:
Medicine Women

From their eighteenth century beginnings, American medical schools were closed to women. Harvard Medical School, founded by three men in 1782, was open to men only.

As a young girl, Harriot K. Hunt was educated in private schools. She became a teacher and opened her own school in 1827. She was interested in medicine but was unable to attend medical school; as was her brother who earned his MD.

Lucretia Mott and her husband, who shared a medical practice, treated Harriot's sister in 1833. Mott was the first woman Hunt had seen practicing as a physician. She immediately began studying medicine independently and became a medical practitioner who treated women and children.

After thirteen years of practice, in 1847 she became the first woman to apply to a medical school. She petitioned Dr. Oliver Wendell Holms, Harvard dean, to be admitted to attend only lectures. The all-male student body, however, met and drew up resolutions of rejection against her stating they were opposed to having the presence of a female in their lecture rooms forced upon them. Their force was greater than that of the dean and Harvard refused her.

Three years later, emboldened by the breakthroughs following the 1848 Women's Rights Convention in Seneca Falls, New York, Hunt again petitioned Holms and was successful. However, before she attended any lecture, the male students gathered in protest. Leading members of the faculty met with Hunt and convinced her to reconsider.

Her further and numerous attempts throughout the Northeast did not merit her admission to any medical school. She continued as a homeopathic physician and became a professor of midwifery and of diseases of women and children at Rochester College. In 1853, she received an honorary degree from the Woman's Medical College of Pennsylvania.

In her 1856 book, *Glances and Glimpses: Or, Fifty Years' Social, Including Twenty Years' Professional Life,* Hunt writes of her inner sorrow at being rejected by Harvard, depriving her of knowledge. This book now sits on a shelf in the Schlesinger Library at Harvard University Medical College.

Dr. Elizabeth Blackwell too had been refused admission to several medical schools because of her gender, but she found acceptance at The Geneva College of Medicine, a small school in upstate New York. But hers was a hate-filled acceptance process that began with the dean of the college.

He presented Blackwell's application directly to his students to decide whether a woman should be allowed to enter classes. He stipulated their decision would have to be unanimous, which he was confident would result in a negative verdict. The students, however, decided it would be a great joke and unanimously voted to admit her. Blackwell bravely sat in classrooms filled with these male students.

Anticipated, unruly incidents at the lectures did not occur, but a genuine respect between the jokester male students and their female colleague did. When asked to absent herself from the lecture on the anatomy of the male reproductive system, Blackwell refused and earned sincere support from her *fellow* students. She passed the qualifying examination with the highest average and graduated in 1849 as Dr. Elizabeth Blackwell, MD, the first American woman to receive a formal medical degree.

Her sister, Dr. Emily Blackwell, MD also had encountered opposition to her medical education achievements. Although accepted to Rush Medical College in Chicago, the all-male Illinois State Medical Society prevented her from completing her studies there. She earned her degree at The Cleveland Medical College.

Other women to be of the first to earn MD degrees were Dr. Mary Harris Thompson and Dr. Marie Zakrzewska. Dr. Thompson, America's first female surgeon, founded the Chicago Hospital for Women and Children and helped organize a college for the medical education of women. Dr. Zakrzewska developed the concept of maintaining medical records. The doctors Elizabeth and Emily Blackwell and Zakrzewska opened the New York Infirmary for Women and Children in 1857, the first hospital in the United States operated by women.

Acceptance of women into the male-medical profession proved to be far off, far into the twentieth century.

Patsy Mink wanted to be a doctor, and in 1948 she was well prepared for medical school with dual undergraduate degrees in zoology and chemistry, or so she thought. Mink applied to twenty medical schools. None accepted women. Mink decided to attend law school to adjudicate this gender injustice. She obtained her JD in 1951 as the only woman in her graduating class at the University of Chicago. During her career as an elected US Representative from the state of Hawaii (1965–2002), Mink coauthored the landmark Title IX legislation.

Born in 1951, little Suze always thought she was going to be a doctor. Her cousin Jolene was born autistic, and from an early age, Suze wanted to fix Jolene's brain. She would pretend to operate on her dolls, cutting into their heads. At thirteen, she became a candy striper in Chicago's Michael Reese Hospital where she could volunteer whenever she chose. When her father was hospitalized with burns he suffered in a fire, Suze pretended to be his doctor.

In 1969, when she met with her college counselor and said she wanted to be a brain surgeon, the counselor said, "Women aren't doctors. Women are nurses," and would not sign off on her premedical courses. Suze majored in social work.

The adult Suze, who could have been one of the best doctors, if not one of the best brain surgeons, went on to become one of the best, if not *the* best financial brain doctor to millions of people whose financial and thus, their physical lives have been saved by Suze Orman.

Note: 1945 - Harvard Medical School admits women.

1975 - Harvard admits women to all schools.

Sources: MORE July/August 2005; http://www.homeoint.org/cazalet/histo/pennsylvfem.htm;
http://www.healthguidance.org/entry/6355/1/Medical-History--Women-in-Medicine.html.
April 2010

Chapter Fifty-two:
Her Cell Phone

~

*C*alled one of the most beautiful women of all time, she changed the way we all call, text, or e-mail for all time to come. She was a glamorous 1940s Hollywood movie star cast in sultry roles by male moviemakers of the decade. However, she also was a polymath with a high IQ.

During that same decade, she patented frequency hopping, a highly efficient way of using multiple radio frequencies simultaneously without interference. It is the basic technology of all wireless communications including cell phones, faxes, bar code scanners, computers, e-mail, the Internet, etc. Today it is known as spread spectrum, but in the 1940s, no one was interested.

Hedy Lamarr (Hedwig Eva Maria Kiesler) was born into a wealthy Jewish family in 1913 Vienna. Her mother was a concert pianist, her father a bank director. Hedwig studied piano and ballet at age ten. She attended finishing school and studied theater in Berlin. But it was the new technology of the cinema that captivated her. She dropped out of school at sixteen and began her career with a bit role in a German movie. Her (scandalous at the time) performance in the 1933 film *Ekstase* received international but notorious attention.

She married Austrian arms manufacturer and millionaire Fritz Mandl when she was just nineteen. She was his trophy wife. He had her accompany him almost everywhere, even to his meetings with arms technicians and his business partners where she heard discussions about advanced technology to be used in weaponry for the pending Nazi war.

But by 1937, she had heard enough. She grew to hate the Nazis as well as her domineering husband. She walked out on her husband, escaped to

Paris, received a divorce, and moved to London. She left behind wealth and a promising film career but kept with her, her detest for the Nazis and the war that was brewing in her homeland.

In London, she met Russian-born American Metro-Goldwyn-Mayer film producer Louis B. Mayer who was well aware of her and her notoriety. He was a prude when it came to his studio's films, but any moral concerns he may have had seemed to override the money that he knew her notoriety would bring into the studio. He gave her a Hollywood movie contract, changed her name, and supposedly insisted she make wholesome films. Hollywood, however, continued to cast her in seductive roles where she seemed to feel uncomfortable. She is quoted to have said, "Any girl can be glamorous. All she has to do is stand still and look stupid."

In Hollywood, Lamarr met American composer George Antheil who had an earlier European music career. He moved to Hollywood to write film scores where he also wrote for *Esquire* magazine. He was notorious due to his avant-garde machinelike, rhythmically propulsive compositions and was dubbed, "the bad boy of music." But he was a musical Picasso. His French *Ballet Mécanique* for percussion ensemble included airplane propellers, electric bells, and a siren. It broke with convention and created uproar at its 1927 American premiere at Carnegie Hall.

Antheil, as Lamarr, was a polymath. They were neighbors who engaged in technical discussions including war weaponry and the pending war. In a 1939 article for *Esquire*, he accurately described the direction the pending war in Europe would take.

In 1940, as they were playing notes on a piano, they were changing keys in unison when Lamarr realized they were talking to each other over a range of tones each separate from the other. She knew at that moment that if translated into radio frequencies to be used in war, it would keep the enemy from locking onto a signal and jamming it.

They sought advice from an electrical engineering professor at the California Institute of Technology and worked for months on a sophisticated anti-jamming device that could be used in radio-controlled torpedoes. In 1942, Lamarr, just twenty-six and Antheil were jointly awarded the US Patent Number 2,292,387 for their Secret Communications System. They donated it as their contribution to the war effort. Antheil later credited the original idea and patent entirely to Lamarr.

The United States formed the National Inventions Council and Lamarr requested a volunteer position. However, neither her invention nor her intelligence would be implemented during World War II. The US military men in power thought she could better help the war effort by selling war bonds for which they used her beauty and her sexy persona. And they proved to be right. She sold millions of dollars worth of war bonds. But history also proved them wrong not to have used her intelligence.

Twenty years hence, during the Cuban Missile Crisis, her invention, using the transistor technology of the late 1950s, was installed on ships sent to blockade Cuba in 1962, three years after her patent expired. Today, her Secret Communications System is used extensively in military communications and for all wireless devices now commonplace.

Neither Lamarr nor Antheil, who died in 1959, received recognition, compensation, or thanks until 1997 when they were awarded the Electronic Frontier Foundation Pioneer Award. Lamarr became the first female recipient of the prized BULBIE Gnass Spirit of Achievement Bronze Award (the Oscar of inventing) given to individuals whose creative lifetime achievements in the arts, sciences, business, or invention fields have significantly contributed to society or the earth at large—literally the World Wide Web.

As her beauty waned so did her movie roles and Lamarr woefully lived out her later years. After her death in 2000 at age eighty-five, according to her wishes, her ashes were spread (spectrumly) in the Vienna Woods air sans cell phone interference.

Sources: *Feminine Ingenuity: Women & Invention in America*, Anne L. Macdonald; "Brainy Beauty," Ron Grossman, *Chicago Tribune*, 3/31/97; www.german-way.com/cinema/bio-hedy-lamarr.html; http://www.inventionconvention.com/americasinventor/dec97issue/section2.html.

Suggested reading: *Spread Spectrum:Hedy Lamarr and the Mobile Phone*, Rob Walters.
June 2010

Conclusion

~

S o why have I written these columns and why have you read them? And why is it important that I have written these columns, and why is it important that you have read them? Because.

Because when we do not recognize historic contributions of women, women may as well be invisible, shrouded, veiled, covered, *femme covert*, buried, however you wish to say it. But they are not.

Because when we do not recognize historic contributions of women, we may think they have not been there or done that, when they have been there and done that. We often just did not know it.

Because when we just did not know it, we often questioned if it was all right to be there again, to do that again, and again and again.

And so in conclusion, I wish to assert, in my audacity of confidence, that you are a different woman than the woman you were before reading *A Thesaurus of Women*.

And I dare to hold, dear, that reading about women who were told they could not, should not, would not dare, because they were women, but did because they were women who did not let gender obstacles stand in their way, has proven to be a positive, informative, inspiring, and empowering experience for you.

And thus, I dare to believe that the steps women took to step over, above, and/or beyond the gender obstacles noted in these chapters will be your guide to step in kind.

Make your own women's history in any way you choose, big or small, personal or public, tangible or intangible, a her history to guide other women then to step in kind with you.

Thank you for taking the time to read your history.

Respectfully,
hjz

Thanks to Women

~

APGAR Score
Birth Certificate Documentation
Boom Mike
Brassiere
Brooklyn Bridge
Brown Paper Bag
Cell Phones
Cherry Blossoms in DC
Child Labor Laws
Computer Language
DNA
Desegregated Buses
Desegregated DNC
Desegregated Little Rock High
  School
E=mc2
Egg Carton
Environmental Movement
E. T. Extraterrestrial Pulsars
FDA
First Demographic Social Survey
Give me your tired ...
Harry Potter
Hearst Castle
International Women's Day
Juvenile Court
Mandatory School Attendance

Montgomery Bus Boycott
NAACP
National Antilynching Campaign
National Consumers League
Nineteenth Amendment
Nuclear Fission
Nursing Education
OSHA
Pie Chart Graphic
Safe Food Storage
Safe WWII Aircraft
Social Security
Social Settlement Houses
Star Distances
Title IX
US Children's Bureau
US Consumer League
www.everythingwireless

Recommended Reading

~

Anne Morrow Lindbergh: First Lady of the Air
    Kathleen C. Winters
Backlash: An Undeclared War Against American Women
    Susan Faludi
Coretta Scott King: A Biography
    Laura T. McCarty
Einstein's Daughter: The Search for Lieserl
    Michele Zackheim
Einstein in Love: A Scientific Romance
    Dennis Overbye
Fast Women: The Drivers Who Changed the Face of Motor Racing
    John Bullock
Freedom's Daughters:
    The Unsung Heroines of the Civil Rights Movement from 1830 to 1970
    Lynne Olson
Hawaii's Story
    Queen Liliuokalani
Looking for Lovedu
    Ann Jones
Male Menopause
    Jed Diamond
Manhood in America: A Cultural History
    Michael Kimmel
Rosalind Franklin: The Dark Lady of DNA
    Brenda Maddox
Silent Spring
    Rachel Carson

Spread Spectrum: Hedy Lamarr and the Mobile Phone
Rob Walters
The Feminine Mystique
Betty Friedan
The Mercury 13
Martha Ackmann
The Montgomery Bus Boycott and the Women Who Started It:
Memoir of Jo Ann Gibson Robinson
Jo Ann Robinson
Twenty Years at Hull House
Jane Addams
Who Cooked the Last Supper?: The Women's History of the World
Rosalind Miles
Women in the Civil Rights Movement: Trailblazers & Torchbearers 1941–1965
Eds. Vicki L Crawford, Jacqueline Anne Rouse, and Barbara Woods